BIBLES &
BATTLE DRUMS

TRUETT ROGERS

BIBLES &
BATTLE DRUMS

JUDSON PRESS
Valley Forge

BIBLES AND BATTLE DRUMS

Copyright © 1976
Judson Press, Valley Forge, PA 19481

Library of Congress Cataloging in Publication Data

Rogers, Truett.
  Bibles and battle drums.

  Bibliography: p. 157
  1. Jones, David, 1736-1820. I. Title.
BX6495.J54R63   286'.1'0924 [B]   75-38193
ISBN 0-8170-0699-0

Printed in the U.S.A.   ⊕

Photo credits: The Frontispiece and photographs on pages 89 and 96 are by Ed Bonner; photographs on pages 21, 30, 55, 69, 82, 124, and 154 are by Joe Essington.

Nullatenus Nequiquam

While writing this book during the past two years, I was, and continue to be, indebted to several special persons:

My wife, Yvonne, voluntarily gave up more personal possessions and contributed more loving understanding than most women give in a lifetime;

my mother, Mary O'Bryan Rogers, a writer herself, was my spiritual physician, confidante, and helper;

my children, Paula, Gary, and Greg, each stood with me when I needed them the most;

my brother, Herschel, provided a home and friendship during my research;

and my friends, Sandy and Betty Belcher, cared for one of my loved ones when I could not.

To each of these this book is affectionately dedicated.

Contents

1

The Welsh Tract

David Jones stood beside General Wayne, waiting. It was hot inside the small tent. He wondered what the message was that had just come from General Washington. That it was important, there was no doubt, for General Wayne looked serious as he spoke with Major Dickens; that it promised action was certain in the way the commanding officer turned to the waiting aide.

"General Washington needs a scout who knows the countryside in Delaware and can report back on the enemy's whereabouts."

David stiffened into attention as he shivered with excitement. "It's my country, sir. I was born there."

General Wayne nodded slowly.

"I've been to school and attended church there, sir. I've fished those creeks and farmed those fields."

General Wayne's long look seemed to be taking in the man from the top of his tricorn to his sturdy boots. His glance rested for a moment on the thickening of the pocket in his tunic that proclaimed a book.

David leaned forward, "Sir, this is land my parents farmed and my grandparents cleared. My own wife and children live but a few miles away." He brought his fist down on the table. "I'll not see the British take it over."

General Wayne's smile was that of a friend, his words those of a commander. "You will accept the duty of a scout and return with the needed information."

David brought his fingertips to his forehead. "It would be a pleasure to serve General Wayne and my native colony as a scout."

"Major Dickens will issue you your identification papers." General Wayne stood and held out his hand to the taller man. "Good hunting, David."

Soon David went to saddle his horse and secure his bedroll to the saddle. His rifle, powder horn, and ammunition pouch were at hand. Most important of all was the small, worn Bible that bulged his pocket. In it he tucked his identification papers, mounted, said a word to his horse, and was off.

As he raced along the dusty road south of Wilmington, he was filled with nostalgia at the familiar sights. He was riding along the road paralleling Christiana Creek which bordered his brother Joshua's farm. This was marshy land where the Christiana was joined by White Clay Creek sweeping from the north, then west to a point just below Wilmington. Since the waterways joined there, the natives duly changed the name of the Christiana from Creek to River. David looked off in the distance and saw the familiar wooded areas along the creek and the flat meadows of farmland. It was good land here. Up north on White Clay Creek the land was dry and chalky, but here it was black with rich, promising texture. His great-grandfather, Morgan Griffith, had been an astute judge of land when he chose the parcel of farm in 1710. Small wonder, he thought, as he rode on, that he had built it into a thriving plantation by the time his sons and daughters divided up the place as their inheritance.

But his thoughts could not be diverted for long from the threat that the British posed both to his ancestry and to his very existence. Only a few miles down the road, there were men who had come to take away his freedom, his family's farms, and even his life as a patriot soldier. He had cut his teeth on resentment of the British. His heritage on both sides of his family was Welsh to the core. Because of persecution by the Church of England, his ancestors had fled to America with other Welshmen who had come to this vast Welsh Tract in search of religious freedom.

Stories of Welsh fights for liberty against English authoritarianism were common after-dinner talk in the old farmhouse when he was a boy. He remembered the tales of Welshman Owen Glendower who single-handedly drove off many of the British lords sent to subject his people, only to lose all his lands once again to later English victories. Even though Wales had become a part of England after the 1530s, its token representation in Parliament had been paid with the price of subtle subjection to the "high English lords and ladies."

It seemed to him that the English were repeating a timeworn pattern of enchaining peoples by coming now to his homeland and attempting to force the colonists to heel to their commands. He

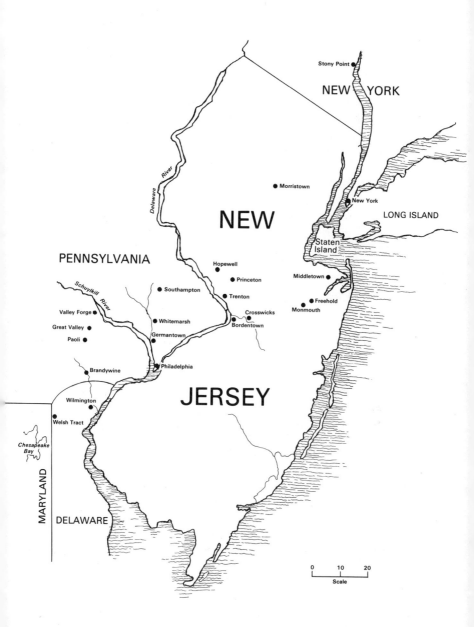

spurred his horse on in a mounting anger and anxiety to join the long ranks of Welshmen who fought the common centuries-old political and religious enemy.

He dismounted at the door of his brother's farmhouse.

"David!" exclaimed his surprised sister-in-law, Sarah. "Oh, David, how are you? Is Ann all right? What's happening, David?" Her words poured forth in a mélange of welcome and anxiety.

"I'm fine, Sarah," he said as he kissed her lightly on the cheek. "I'm here to report to General Washington in order to help find the British. Do you know where the general is? And where is Josh?"

"Joshua has taken a wagonload of our things to Cousin Abel's in Wilmington. We're going there later today. David, will there be a battle here?" Her eyes matched the edginess of her voice in apprehension over the farm and their personal safety.

"I hope not," he said without conviction. "Sarah, Ann begged me to send you to our place. She could use a blood relative nearby with all this uncertainty and confusion. You know we want you to come, don't you?"

"Of course I know that, David, and I'll encourage Joshua to think on it."

David had been shifting from one foot to the other in obvious nervousness due to his anxiety to get to the front lines of the conflict. "Now, where is General Washington?"

"One of the Davis boys rode over yesterday and said he was headquartered on Iron Hill, but that is all we've heard."

David patted her affectionately on the shoulder and swung into his saddle.

"Let me get you something to eat before you go," she pleaded.

"Thanks, but later maybe," he said, as his mind was thinking ahead to his mission. "Now see to your own safety and that of your family, Sarah." With that he was off down the pathway to the road that led to Iron Hill.

An aide-de-camp to the general received David's credentials at the headquarters and then informed him that he was to be given several mounted troopers to scout one sector to the northwest in search of British troops and plans. They were to take prisoners if possible, to avoid any action that might lose men, and to report back as soon as any sightings, news from local inhabitants, or action was taken. He was to travel lightly. Did he have a pistol? When he said that he did not, he was dispatched to supply for a weapon and any other equipment he deemed necessary. A runner was sent out to one of the units to fetch David six good light-horse cavalry. They were off by midafternoon, with David in his first command, seeking out the enemy. Neither the novelty of command nor the stimulation of imminent combat could deter the single-minded hatred he possessed in his heart for those in red coats somewhere off in the distance.

The afternoon was spent stopping at various farms of old family friends for information. If they had known David's family and had, perhaps, gone to the Welsh Tract Baptist Church with the Joneses, David felt he could trust them not to be some of those British-sympathizing Americans called Tories. He was aware that it was hot. His wife, Ann, had knitted a handsome sweater for last year's campaign on the upper Hudson at Ticonderoga and Crown Point. "Too handsome," he had muttered, "to fight a war in." It had been cool earlier in the morning, but the sun had washed away the milky haze of dawn by this time. Now the sun was hot on his back as perspiration trickled down his shoulders and arms. He did not stop to take off the sweater now, though, for he was on an errand of such magnitude that nothing could slow his determination to halt the British. No enemy was seen that afternoon, however, and David felt that the afternoon of August 30, 1777, was frustratingly fruitless.

The next two days proved to be monotonous and disappointing, for no contact was made with the enemy and precious little positive information was forthcoming as to their whereabouts. Where the British had not been was about all that David had determined. September 2 was a different day, however, as the patrol stumbled almost into the lap of some enemy light cavalry who, like David, were carefully searching out the countryside.

They were passing through a narrow pathway in a thicket of woods when David saw the red coats of a small detachment of six to eight British troopers loom suddenly in front of him.

"To the left, quickly!" David shouted as he pulled his horse away from the enemy. His reaction was instantaneous, but even as he made his movement, his brain subconsciously flashed a signal from his memory that there was a swampy area to his right where he remembered being stuck in a family wagon as a boy. Both units scattered unmolested into the safe, shadowy depths of the forest without a shot being fired. Even as David turned his horse, though, he was exhilarated with the knowledge that he might well have the British trapped.

As the men gathered around David, he talked low and fast: "There's a swamp in front of them now, and their only hope to escape is to go back up the edge of the road where they came. You two men get up there quickly and cut off that road." He waved his hand in the desired direction and the two men moved out quickly.

David's eyes were wide, but the countenance of his face was that of one expecting something exciting to happen in his favor. "You two cover the opposite way, now, and we'll come to you if we hear firing." The flankers moved out, and David and the remaining two cavalrymen waited nervously for them to disappear in the brush.

Now David spoke in a slow, deliberate voice that promised a determined climax to the confrontation. "Cock your pistols, men, and each man charge straight ahead. Do not fire until you are sure to hit your target." With pistol cocked and held upward and high, David spurred his horse forward and the charge was on. Twigs snapped, branches were hurled aside, and the sound of pounding hooves excited horses and men to greater speed and readiness.

"There they are!" The shout came from the man on David's far left, but all they got was a brief glimpse of two Britishers far ahead in the swamp and heading away from them deep in muddy water. Pursuit did not turn up a single enemy. He returned to the staging area empty-handed and to the news that the British were packing up and readying for a move toward the Christiana.

September 3 found David up before dawn. General Washington had sent most of his troops to Red Clay Creek to attempt battle, but he had wisely left about seven hundred men under Brigadier General William Maxwell stationed along Christiana Creek in case the enemy should approach from the direction south of Iron Hill. It was soon obvious that the main British force was headed, not for Red Clay Creek, but for the small force left to guard the flank at Christiana Creek. General Maxwell posted his men up the hill, on the sides of the road, in the trees, and behind rocks and makeshift barricades as the enemy came at the ready.

As the shots intensified, and small, scattered skirmishes grew into a full-fledged battle, a small detachment arrived from Philadelphia to bring support. Even more meaningful than the muskets was the flag carried by the man marching at the head of the company. Here, for the first time, was the flag that had been adopted by Congress on June 14, 1777. It was a small flag, as were all regimental banners, but this flag represented all the colonies, and not individual units, like the popular Rhode Island standard. This flag had thirteen stripes of alternating red and white, as had earlier flags carried by military units, but in the upper left-hand corner was a blue field with a circle of thirteen white stars. Those stars were in sharp contrast to earlier versions of colonial banners which had a small Union Jack to complement the red and white stripes.

David's heart quickened when he saw the standard, for he could tell at a glance that this was a colonial banner without trace of the British Union Jack, and that made it good enough for him. These were the "Stars and Stripes" he had heard about when passing through Philadelphia on his way to Delaware, and the surge of excitement he felt knew no bounds. The sounds of shots to the east, however, interrupted his thoughts, and he rode off in pursuit of the headquarters detachment which was now moving to higher ground for a better view.

When they reached a place that afforded them a fair angle of the skirmish in the distance, they saw their troops falling back in front of a bayonet charge following a brief stand at the bridge near Thomas Cooch's house. General Maxwell turned his horse to face the runners, the men who rode with his commands to the various units, and shouted forth his orders in a loud, sharp torrent of words: "Tell the company commanders to use harassing methods only. No frontal stand is to be made until we have fallen back north toward Ogleton Road. Get the fieldpieces across that creek yonder," he waved a hand north toward Persimmon Creek, "and get these pieces across the bridge before any infantry is allowed to cross."

The turning of his horse's head and spurring his mount down the hill was the signal for the messengers to dash off with their instructions. David, by prearrangement, headed for the First Pennsylvanians, Captain Joseph McClure, commander.

By the time David joined the Continentals, they had formed an ambuscade across the Newark-Welsh Tract Road junction. Hoping to surprise the British and to allow more time for the colonists to retreat toward General Washington's troops behind them on Red Clay Creek, they were forming a line fairly well hidden in trees, in the depression of Persimmon Creek, and by the Welsh Tract Baptist Church. Most of the troops were following the artillery pieces northward while those readying for the arrival of the British cocked their rifles and muskets and set themselves grimly into position.

David was riding to the church to see if he might help with the wounded when his horse pitched straight upward and almost threw him. A British cannonball passed through the church as he reined up to stop. David grew livid with rage. This was the church of his childhood. He had attended school here and accompanied his brothers and sisters when they buried his mother and father, who were lying now under the rushing feet of the Continental soldiers scurrying back to the road. His brother, Zachariah, only about a year older than he, had been buried less than two months before beside his parents in the northeast corner of the churchyard.

Was there to be no limit to the outrages he was to suffer at the hands of these marauding criminals? Would the old homeplace burn beneath their torches this night? Perhaps, he thought, he himself would fall a victim to their vicious attacks. Somehow, with the hot blood of anger pumping in his veins, he really didn't care if he did die.

Confusion reigned now. Shouts were raised that a cavalry troop of British had swung eastward to cut off their escape toward White Clay and Red Clay creeks. Then the angry sounds of personal combat arose—cracking rifles, the screams of wounded and dying men, neighing horses, crashing cannons, running, shuffling men with terror the hallmark of every facial expression.

David did his best to pass on the word that the troopers should head east along Ogleton Road. Soon it became obvious that the battle was over. The British were not pursuing, and the colonists were searching for a suitable place to camp along White Clay Creek. The British had gotten bogged down in Purgatory Swamp and had pulled back toward Cooch's Bridge for the night. No more threats of attack faced the tired, bone-weary troops. This day's fighting was over.

Since David was assigned to no specific unit, he left word with General Maxwell's second-in-command that he would report tomorrow to headquarters. He then swung his horse past wagons bearing the dead bodies of what appeared to be several dozen Continental and British soldiers. His training as a surgeon and the bloodshed of the day reminded him that he simply must see if he could help the doctors. He followed the wagons to a tent on the bank of White Clay Creek and assisted the surgeon in charge with the few cases that required amputation and bandaging.

Now, physically exhausted, he headed his horse past the camps of sleeping troops and arrived at his brother Joshua's farm. Sarah and the children were gone, but Joshua was there and roused to greet David. After a brief report from David concerning the day's fighting, both men realized that they had had nothing to eat since a bit of dried meat for breakfast in the early morning hours. Though hungry, tired, and nervous about the close proximity of the British, the two brothers found some bread, took a drink from the well, and soon were fast asleep.

Who was this David Jones? He was David Jones of Chester County, Pennsylvania. Was he a young man itching for battle like a two-year-old stallion attempting to burst out of his paddock? No, he was forty-one years old and a settled family man. Was he a politically motivated member of a Pennsylvania Committee of Correspondence? No, he was a Baptist minister on leave from his church to fight the British. Was he an aide-de-camp to General Anthony Wayne? No, he was only recently made a chaplain to General Wayne's brigade, and he was to follow his commander through Brandywine to Valley Forge, Yorktown, and beyond. Was he a part-time physician with a medical degree? No, he was a talented student of medical surgery who had studied and practiced under two prominent New Jersey doctors in the 1760s. Was the chaplaincy to be David's single claim to fame? Not at all. He would prove to be a competent pastor, a learned theologian and writer, a concerned missionary to the Indians, and an enthusiastic organizer of Baptist churches.

In 1746, the new church building was bathed in sunlight and freshened with paint, awaiting the coming of the people for a day of dedication and fellowship. The Baptist meetinghouse at Welsh Tract was the pride and joy of its people. For years, they had met in the old frame building, built in 1707, that leaked rain, was cold in the winter, and let in wind and stifling heat in the summer. But now, standing proudly amid the Delaware countryside, the new edifice was the result of years of sacrificial labor, giving, and hope.

The religious fervor of the early 1740s had left its mark here, as elsewhere, in the American colonies. In 1741, when George Whitefield had come to the area, great crowds and much emotional display had ensued. This "Great Awakening," led by Whitefield and Jonathan Edwards, did not usher in a new religious dawn for all mankind, as many had prophesied, but it did encourage many to find a new relationship with God and their fellowmen through existing churches. Welsh Tract Baptist Church was one of those groups reaping the benefits of the religious revival.

The meetinghouse was designed as a one-story, hipped-roof building of bricks imported from England and Wales, laid in Flemish bond. Some of the rocks used on the porch steps had been gathered from the creekbeds nearby. Greenish-brown moss clung to the sides of the steps this morning, glistening in the sunlight.

The Baptist meetinghouse began its silent welcome of the members who came in wagons and on horseback. Many, choosing to enjoy the summer morning to the fullest, walked. It was early morning, and the mist had not, as yet, been burned off by the sun. The sky was cloudless, however, promising a lovely day. The Davis family came slowly down Iron Hill Road with their wagon wheels crunching the dirt, throwing up only a little dust. The wagon was packed with every dish of food for which Mary, the mother and wife, had been so highly praised in the past. The children, failing to tolerate the slow pace of the horse-drawn wagon, jumped down laughing, shouting, and running pell-mell for the meadow and the stream beyond it to the north. The Morgans heard the happy excitement before they caught the meetinghouse in their view as they moved up old Welsh Tract Road. Others were nearing the site for the day of thanksgiving, praise, fellowship, and dedication of the Welsh Tract Baptist Church this early Sunday morning, July 19, 1746.

Morgan Jones and his wife, Eleanor, were late, however. Morgan was out hitching up their most dependable horse, Clink, to the wagon. Eleanor, though, was fuming as she walked down the back meadow toward the creek. Beads of perspiration stood out on her forehead and arms from the exertion of walking in the warming sunshine.

"Jos! Dafydd! Sech! Ble mae'r bechgyn?"[1] Of all the times for them to be gone! "This is what I might have expected of David and Zach, but Joshua is old enough to be where he is supposed to be." She called again, "Joshua! Zach! David!" In exasperation, hitching up her skirt with both hands, she stormed back toward the house to

---

[1] "Josh! David! Zach! Where are those boys?" Almost all the families of Welsh Tract spoke Welsh as their only language in the eighteenth century. The Welsh Tract Baptist Church conducted its services in Welsh until about 1800, and David used English as his primary language only when he left home for school in 1758.

tell their father. She did not enjoy turning their father's wrath on them for being gone, but they deserved some kind of punishment for their absence at such an important time.

"Are you ready, Eleanor?" Morgan said pleasantly, smiling to his wife as she approached. Her frown and frustration erased the smile from his face. "What's the matter?" he inquired.

"It's your boys," she answered curtly, as if they were his and not hers. "Joshua, Zach, and David are gone, and I can't find them anywhere. John, Morgan, and the girls are all here, but not those three. I just can't understand Josh, as old as he is, being gone, and I'm sure the younger boys are with him."

"Oh, is that all?" Morgan said, turning back to the horses. "They asked me if they could ride over to Iron Hill on their way to church."

"What?" she snapped. "Why didn't you tell me?"

"Well, since it's such a special day, and so nice and sunny, I thought it would be all right. I asked Josh to see that Zach and David didn't ruin their church clothes."

Eleanor ran her hands along the sides of her hair, bound in a tight bun at the back, to be sure she hadn't ruined her combing. Satisfied that she had not, and exasperated with her husband for not informing her of the boys' disappearance, she turned sharply and stepped quickly toward the house without another word.

Joshua had certainly tried to keep the younger boys fairly clean, but he had failed with David. David had taken off his Sunday shoes and knee stockings before he left the barn, holding them in his hands as he mounted one of the two horses behind Zach. But now at the entrance of the old, abandoned iron mine, temptation had gotten the better of him. The sound of dripping water inside the tunnel inexorably drew him into its dark cavern. He climbed over the forbidden barrier to the tunnel's entrance and knelt on hands and knees beside the small pool of water made by the dripping of some unseen spring deep within the hill. As he pushed a small stick into the water, his imagination created the white sail and smooth breezes of ships and sailors he had so often seen on the Delaware River just a few miles to the east. What he should have seen was that his Sunday shirt was wet to the elbows.

Josh's voice broke the concentration on his sailing ventures, "Davey, come on out! You know good and well that Mum will skin you alive, and me, too, if you get messy."

The mouth of the tunnel had been barricaded for years, ever since the early Welsh miners had dug for iron here over twenty years ago. All of the boys knew that they were not to go in there, ever. Ten-year-old Davey Jones peered out of the top of the tunnel and began stepping barefooted and very gingerly down the sharp rocks and logs to the flat surface near his older brothers.

"Davey, your shirt is wet!" said Josh in anguish. "Now take it off and maybe it will get dry on the way to church. Gosh, Davey, can't you stay out of that mine? You know that Pa has whupped you more than once for getting in there, and besides, you always get dirty when you go in." Twenty-year-old Josh was a stout, short young man with long hair pulled back behind his head.

Davey respected his age, size, and strength, but he didn't feel like being "fathered" by his older brother today. He showed his displeasure at being treated like the ten-year-old that he was by saying, "If you have me take off any more clothes, Josh, I'll be naked. Come on, I want to ride to the top."

"Davey!" Josh spoke sharply. "Take off your shirt!"

Davey took it off.

The boys saw their family wagon as they arrived at the point just east of the church. The wagon was hitched up in one of the newly covered stalls on the far side of the road near the parsonage. Davey and Zach dismounted in the woods while Davey dressed, and then they joined some of their friends down by the creek, carefully avoiding their "Mum" until Davey's shirt had had a chance to dry. Morgan and Eleanor were exchanging greetings with friends and relatives in that warm glow of happinesss that comes when one is with those special people who are loved and enjoyed. Morgan stood with a small group of men near the front door of the church, inspecting the work of carpenters and masons who had only the night before put the finishing touches on their work.

Morgan was a quiet man, short, stocky, and dependable in all he did. He had not been a Christian for most of his fifty-eight years, as had most of the other men who talked animatedly about the construction. His wife had married him while he was still not a Christian, though he was morally strong and likable. However, with his strong Christian family roots, and with much love and understanding mixed with patience from Eleanor, Morgan had come on his own to Pastor Davis three years before and asked to be instructed on how to express his faith in the Baptist way. His

profession of faith and baptism had pleased not only the family, but also the entire community, for everyone highly respected this good solid neighbor and friend.

In spite of Morgan's obvious stability, however, it was Eleanor who led the family in most ways. She had that indirect, gentle, feminine manner which allowed her to work her will without being known as an unsubmissive wife. She was not from one of the first families that had made an early niche in the life of the Welsh Tract community. Her forefathers had only recently sailed for America to join those of Morgan's family who had earlier, with other Welshmen, purchased the thirty-thousand-acre tract from William Penn. She was intelligent, loving, firm, and consistent in her relationships with her family as well as with her friends. She had felt a bit uncomfortable in their first years of marriage because of the comparison of her relatively poor heritage with Morgan's more affluent parentage. However, her personality and native Welsh background soon earned her a solid reputation in the community. They had taken over a good farm inherited by Morgan from his parents, and they continued to develop the land with hard work and good management. They had had nine living, healthy children. Two others had died in infancy. All in all, they had a good life.

The bell on the new steeple broke the conversations and called the people to study and worship. The Bible classes met by ages, and the younger children met outside in the shade of the big trees on warm, sunny days like this one. At 10:00 A.M. the congregation gathered for its first worship service in the new building. Welshmen joined their voices in singing the slow, melodic praises to their God. They used no instruments to accompany them, and few of them could read musical notes. Yet they sang in four-part harmony that created a reverent attitude, drawing them close to God and to one another. Prayers were long, as usual, but today everyone noticed that there was a bit more intensity on the part of the deacons as they prayed; their gratitude to God for what he had wrought in the form of this meetinghouse was felt deeply in the breast of every member, child, and visitor present.

The people settled into the pews with a rustle following a hymn, and a reverent silence ensued as the pastor and one of the deacons stepped down into the front pew and assisted the venerable Enoch Griffith to the pulpit. Mr. Griffith had been an organizer of the expedition when the second large group from Wales sailed for the Welsh Tract in 1710. David's father and grandfather had been a part of that group. Mr. Griffith had sacrificed personally in order that others might have the better land in the valley; yet he had built a fine farm, reared six fine children, and was one of the original deacons of the Baptist fellowship.

This older, stout man, assisted by the two younger men, moved slowly up the steep steps into the pulpit, mounted high above the first row of seats. The cane in his right hand was the same one he used to hobble around the fields, but his coat was of fine material, black and buttoned all the way to his neck. His white lace cravat, attached to his shirt, was crushed a bit by the buttoning of his coat, but he was well dressed for the occasion. In his left hand he held several sheets of paper. He gripped the pulpit corners for a moment and looked out over the parishioners, accustoming himself to this strange position for a layman. He adjusted the papers and his spectacles, and then began his short, but pointed, address.

"If we would understand our present drift and the lines upon which we, as a people, are moving socially, religiously, and morally, we must study that portion of our history which preceded us. We were called the 'Emigrant Church' because so many of us set foot on these shores in the year of our Lord, 1710. The Morgans, the

Griffiths, the Joneses, the Lewises, the Evanses, the Davises—these were the founders, the builders, the strength and stay of what we now are. It was then that the ideals we hold, consciously or unconsciously, were wrought into the very inner nature of our souls." His message was that of remembrance, of history, of forefathers buried outside in the cemetery, and of a challenge to build in the future on what had transpired in the past.

Pastor Davis mounted the pulpit next and read the Scripture from Exodus 40:33-35: "And he reared up the court round about the tabernacle and the altar, and set up the hanging of the court gate. So Moses finished the work. Then a cloud covered the tent of the congregation, and the glory of the Lord filled the tabernacle." He closed the Bible and began to speak. "This day we, too, have finished the work. Men and women, faithful to their Creator, have dealt faithfully with God's business. With the labor of our own hands we have erected a meetinghouse to the glory of God. Here we shall marry the young and bury the dead. Here we shall sing, pray, teach, worship, and fellowship. Through it all we, too, should the Almighty Sovereign so deign, shall see the glory of the Lord enter this place."

The pastor's usual droning monotony was absent this day. Instead, a crispness marked his words, and an earnestness characterized the tone and mannerisms of all present. Even ten-year-old David Jones' attention was drawn to the proceedings and held without distraction, an unusual occurrence for him.

At last Pastor Davis closed the sermon, and there followed a time of prayer at the altar. The deacons and visiting pastors gathered, and while all knelt, one of their own, young Abel Morgan of Middletown, New Jersey, offered the prayer of dedication. After the prayer, an iron plate from the old mine on Iron Hill with the name of the church and the date was presented to the pastor for the purpose of bolting it to the cornerstone at a later time.

As the service concluded, excited children and contented adults spilled out of the new building to the long rows of tables, laid out prior to the service, and began loading the boards laid on kegs and sawhorses until they sagged beneath the weight of beautiful, delectable food. Fresh corn, beans, lettuce, strawberries, potatoes, greens, blackberries, carrots, and pickles gave way down the tables to roast beef, pork, and special dishes brought by cooks with talent and experience. Davey's eyes fairly bulged as he anxiously awaited his plate and utensils. The men lined up first—the pastor, deacons, and visitors, then the other men. At last, the women and children were motioned over. Eleanor gathered her children around her, issuing out items of tableware.

"Davey, your shirt's been mussed. Oh, Davey, please, please be careful. We have another service this afternoon." She shot a darting glance toward Josh, but he merely shrugged his shoulders in a gesture of helplessness.

The days passed quickly for David, as he kept busy working on the farm and going to school. His father was not an exceptionally hard taskmaster, but he laid out a long schedule of work and expected all in the family to do their share. Each share was a large one, for they were raising ninety acres of corn, feed for the livestock, and, in addition, near the house a large garden of vegetables and fruit which was to feed the family throughout the year. A few head of cattle, pigs, chickens, and goats had to be cared for in addition to the household chores. The Joneses lived in a rectangular, two-story frame house. It was a fairly large house for that time and that section of the colony. Though it was large, it was rather plain, for while they had inherited a large farm, they had not come into great wealth as had some of their neighbors farther down the county in Sussex. The house was located on a rise of land some three hundred yards north of the Christiana Creek. This part of the countryside was heavily wooded, so much so in fact that the streams in the area sometimes had a touching canopy of trees formed over them by the overhanging branches on each side of the bank. The cultivated fields still had some stumps in them which had proved too large and deep-rooted for David's father to pull out when the fields were originally cleared for cultivation.

David's older brothers, Joshua and John, worked the fields with their father, while his older sister, Ann, and younger sisters, Esther and Lettice, worked in the house with their mother. David worked with Zachariah and Morgan in the vegetable garden. Zach was only about a year older than David, and Morgan was only thirteen months younger. Since they were so close in age, they were assigned the job nearest the house in order that they could be within sight and hearing of their mother, who managed a fair amount of supervision.

These three boys had as their primary tools a wooden hoe and a push-and-pull plough. Each of the boys preferred the hoe to the plough because of the constant bickering over who would push and who would pull the cumbersome instrument. No two combinations of the three boys could coordinate the proper power from both behind and in front of the plough. Amazingly, the garden prospered in spite of the three boys, and it provided the household with fine, fresh Delaware Valley vegetables.

Since farming was the usual occupation of the families of the Tract, it was only natural that most of the families trained their children to follow in the footsteps of their farmer fathers. David's brothers had, from the beginning, expressed an interest in various sections of the farm that they hoped to have as their own one day, but the size of the land that Morgan owned prohibited its division into too many sections. Morgan, therefore, began to encourage David and Morgan, the two younger boys, to take up other occupations. When he noted that David was particularly skilled with his hands, he attempted to train him as a carpenter. His mother, however, saw something else in David.

Of all the Jones children, only David enjoyed attending the classes at the "Old School Church" as the Welsh Tract Baptist Meetinghouse was commonly called. He did not enjoy the unusual Welsh hornbook, that wide piece of smooth wood on which was placed a faded yellow sheet for writing, doing figures, and spelling. However, if there were a new book introduced to the school, David soon had it at home in the upstairs sleeping loft, reading it by candlelight far into the night. By his teenage years he was reading and understanding some of the Greek classics which had been translated into Welsh. On top of whatever book was currently being read, though, he placed his Welsh-language Bible. Only David accepted from his father the challenge to read through the Bible every year. He could wander alone in the private world of his books as he found both an escape from the drudgery of farm life and a challenge to learn about the larger world around him. The reality of that world was brought home to the Jones family when their second eldest, John, was severely wounded in Braddock's campaign against the French on the western frontier in 1755.

Constant turmoil faced the Delaware residents of the mid-1700s. The French and English had involved the colonists in a military imbroglio for years. Following the Glorious Revolution of 1689, the first of what became known as the Colonial Wars broke out between England and France. The colonists, being loyal subjects of the English Crown, bore their share of the fighting. Again in 1703 and in 1744, the two world powers were at it again, and, as always, the colonists left farm and family to fight the French and their partners, the Indians, hostile to both the English and the colonists.

No sooner had the Treaty of Aix-la-Chapelle been signed in 1748 to end the third conflict than the French sent Céleron de Bienville through the upper Ohio River valley in the summer of 1749 to build a chain of forts from Lake Erie to the forks of the Ohio. The French position was strong in 1752, and Indian raids on outlying settlements began to be a hazard to frontiersmen and isolated farmers all along the Delaware Valley. In April, 1754, the French expelled a Virginia working party from the forks of the Ohio, and Colonel George Washington led a troop of Virginia militia against their centuries-old enemy. However, the French defeated and captured the entire unit in July. General Braddock was then commissioned to clear the French out of the western section of Pennsylvania, and he was to spare no cost or effort to do so. His well-prepared troops were dealt a crushing blow, however, as they approached Fort Duquesne. John Jones was one of the wounded carried back to the Welsh Tract with the news of the disaster. Now, with a fresh defeat from the French, and with the Indians on the warpath in upper New England and western Pennsylvania, the ring was closing fast around frightened Delaware farmers. Eighteen-year-old David Jones joined the local militia unit and prepared for combat.

It was a hot, clear, sunny day along the dusty Glasgow Road as the men began to gather. With Joshua caring for the farm and John recuperating from his wounds, the next two boys in the Jones family reported for training: Zach and David. Morgan was left, to his chagrin, to tend the garden.

David wore a long, white cotton shirt open at the neck and draped over his leather work trousers. His leather leggings were stuffed inside his heavy boots, and his wide-brimmed hat served him well in keeping the sun off his face and neck. His cartridge box and belt along with his powder horn and old "Brown Bess" musket were strapped to his saddle. Most of the other men and boys had already gathered and were standing in the ranks that had been assigned earlier. David tied his horse with the other animals, unlashed his equipment, and took his place with the taller men at the head of the third row.

"Hey, Davey, we're going to do the firing drill today," John

Moale spoke in an excited voice as David fell into the ranks. Beside him, Tom Aiken turned to David, nodded toward a group of officers by the trees in front of the troops, and said, "Yeah, we've got some real regulars who've come, too, and they're going to watch us and see how we do."

David followed his glance and saw amid the older men, who had been elected as officers by the company previously, two bright red uniforms of real British regulars. One of them wore a towering peaked hat and the other a tricorn with feathers. They stood more erect than the militiamen around them, but they said nothing. They simply watched and listened.

Captain Lippincott approached and stood stiffly, but unnaturally for a fellow farmer in the valley. "All men have muskets, powder horn, and cartridge boxes and fall into ranks."

"Oh, my gosh, I left all my stuff with the horse," David heard Zach gasp at the end of the line. Most of the men and boys scurried like scattered chickens to get their equipment. Finally, they started moving back to the place where David continued to stand with a few others who had lined up correctly. The British regulars watched.

"Now, men, the order of firing is this," Captain Lippincott began when all lines were dressed. "Be sure your flint and striker are in good shape. Clear all powder out of the pan, then load on command. First, place your rifle butts on the ground at order arms; second, place a cartridge in the barrel and ram it down with the ramrod. Third, come to ready. Fourth, prime the pan; fifth, come to full cock and wait for the command to fire."

All the men there knew very well how to fire their muskets. They had killed many deer, squirrels, and birds for the family table with their weapons, but they were not accustomed to firing in ranks with others. Expressions of confidence were written on most of the faces as they hurried to show the regulars just how good they were with their weapons.

"All right, together now, first rank take two steps forward and come to attention. Order arms!" he shouted.

Some of the men put their weapons to their sides with the butts on the ground. Others jerked uncertainly, not knowing what to do. Still others looked around and asked quickly and nervously, "Hey, what's going on?"

"Come to order arms, stupid! Put your musket on the ground."

"Why didn't he say put your muskets down, then?" snapped Sam

Fisher. "If he'd get out of the way and shut up, I'd show him how to fire this musket."

"Quiet in the ranks," shouted Lippincott, but the men continued to mutter to one another and to themselves as the orders were given. Someone dropped his powder horn; another fired early. It was mass confusion, a fiasco of order, and most frustrating to the officers, since they knew quite well that these men knew how to fire their weapons and did it well.

The British regulars continued to watch without sign of emotion. Finally, David's rank was ordered forward and the commands began: "Order arms! Load! Ram! At the ready! Prime! Full cock! Fire! Order arms!"

David's group wasn't much better, and Tom Aiken, standing next to David, couldn't keep up with the others. With each command, he was behind. David whispered each command to him before it was shouted, but Tom acted late and uncertainly. Out of the corner of his eyes, David noticed the British regular with the tricorn and feathers approaching behind the line. His face carried a scowl that boded trouble. He soon stood directly behind Tom, and when that militiaman dropped his ramrod, there was a piercing shriek from the regular.

"Fall out of the rank, blockhead!" When Tom leaned over to get the ramrod from the dust, the regular kicked it with his shiny black boot and grabbed Tom's shirt, jerking him off his feet. As he lay there in the dust, he looked up with wide, wild eyes, not knowing what to do next.

"Get over there with the other sluggards, you idiot! You are an inept oaf, and you aren't now and you probably never will be a soldier. You will get yourself and some others killed if we can't whip you into shape. And whip you into shape we will, today." His high screechy voice didn't match the majesty of his beautiful uniform, but he made himself understood.

Tom got up and scrambled toward the small group of men who were being formed into a line by the other regular in the peaked hat. Then, to David's horror, the screaming regular placed his face within inches of his own and shouted, "And you, soldier, will kindly remain silent in ranks. Who gave you permission to instruct these men?"

David was dumbfounded.

"Well, who?"

"No one, sir," David said softly.

"Then keep your mouth shut." With that, he stalked off to join those who received special instruction. David felt crushed, with a sickness in his stomach. His hands shook so badly that he continued to drill only with great difficulty.

By the end of the day, David had been assigned a position with the first rank of men who were adept at following the drill, and Tom, after returning from the redcoats, didn't drop his ramrod again. David waited for the men to disperse after the drill and then made his way over to Captain Lippincott. When they were alone, David spoke earnestly.

"Captain, I'm sorry for talking in ranks today and making the major angry. I hope I didn't get any others in trouble."

"Forget it, Davey," said Lippincott with a pat on David's shoulder. "You think you got a tongue-lashing? You should have heard what old 'featherhead' had to say to me. Besides, he was the one who suggested that you go to the first rank. He said you had the makings of a good soldier." David's face expressed surprise. "Well, that's the army for you, Davey boy."

David rode the three miles home by himself, deep in his own thoughts. It was difficult for him to understand why he liked the army so much. Usually those who wouldn't work on the farms, wouldn't study, and were just plain dissatisfied with their lives and futures went off to the army these days. But David was looking forward to further schooling. He dearly loved to read, and he knew what he wanted to be—a minister. He greatly desired to preach, to be a respected scholar, and to be a professional man like his cousin Abel. But the army? Why did it hold such a fascination for him?

As the weeks passed, it soon became apparent that the Welsh Tract militia was not going to be called into active duty. The tide of the war with the French and Indians was swinging inexorably toward the English, and most of the fighting was to the north. The Welsh Tract militia was only used as a home defense, and there simply wasn't much to defend in that vicinity. More and more, David felt pulled to continue his education and enter the ministry. Discussions with his parents and with Pastor Davis confirmed his feeling that the desire in his heart was tantamount to a call from God.

He professed his faith and was baptized in the summer of 1758. Isaac Eaton had started a Baptist school, an academy, in 1756—the first one of that faith in America. Eaton's Hopewell church and school were also of the Welsh background so familiar to David, and both of his parents encouraged him to attend since there was more than enough help on the farm to do the work. Hopewell, New Jersey, was full of friends, and it was also near cousin Abel and the Middletown congregation where other family friends like the Stillwells lived. He could work for his keep, and his parents gave him some money in case he needed it for some unexpected expense. He determined to go.

In September, 1758, David rode off from the farm with full saddlebags and took a long look down the Christiana Valley. He knew he would be back many times, but in his heart he also felt that he was leaving home to make a new life for himself. He had no pangs of last-minute doubt. His confidence sprang from a confident personality. He was a young man of the soil who had deep roots in a stable community and family life. As such, he found his self-assurance in an inner spiritual strength, and while some of his friends doubted the wisdom of his leaving the security of Welsh Tract, he was wise enough not to govern his life by the expectations of others. Since he desperately desired more schooling, he was sure that the ministry was the correct, God-ordained profession for him. Yet, to leave his mother and father, his brothers and sisters, the church, his friends—it was not an easy moment. But he pointed his horse northward toward Hopewell, school, and a bright, exciting future. He was prepared to enter a new phase of life with a solid family, church, and community background. Failure never entered his mind.

Hopewell Academy

2

Anniefach

"Well, I'm back in the garden again," David thought, as he gathered the last of the potatoes, carrots, and beans. He smiled at his misconception of what he had thought school would be. Instead of a large, imposing professor with deep voice and erudition, his teacher was Rev. Isaac Eaton. The Reverend was, indeed, intelligent, but his frame was small and his voice rough with constant hoarseness. Instead of sitting in large classrooms with fine chalkboards and individual desks, David's class of eight young men sat around a large oval table in the parsonage dining room. Rather than having scholarly discussions around the fireplace, David had to earn his keep by tending the garden, milking two cows, and helping clean the dishes after meals.

The ringing of the bell near the back porch interrupted his thoughts and summoned all the students from their chores to another lesson. For David, the first afternoon class would be theology. He picked up his basket of vegetables and headed for the main house.

"At least this will be easier than the morning," he sighed. As one of the boys ran by him, he called out over his shoulder to David, "Hey, David! Maybe if you did your figures in Welsh, you'd be better at math!"

David didn't smile. Following Latin and Greek in the morning, the math lesson was the last study session prior to lunch. It was a long hour for him. He had never liked to work with figures. When other boys appeared fascinated with the successful results of a complicated mathematical formula, David only shrugged.

"So what?" he had said inadvertently once in the presence of Rev. Isaac Eaton. "Those figures aren't as pretty as a picture, and they certainly aren't as important as the Bible."

"David!" Mr. Eaton spoke sharply. "A minister is to be 'a

workman that needeth not to be ashamed.' You are to do all your work well, and a minister's work is God's work. Therefore, it should be done properly."

David tried to do the figures and formulas correctly, but his real interest lay in the reading subjects and in theology. The theology lesson, to which he now hastened, was his preference, for he enjoyed reading not only the Bible, but also the commentaries written by past and present scholars. He found himself reading the theology books on his own time, but the mathematics and logic were other matters. He understood that reading alone would not suffice to give him a complete education, but the figures and philosophy were slower, more tedious, and much more difficult for him.

David deposited his vegetables in the kitchen and took his seat at the study table with the others. He sat between Sam Jones and James Manning. Both of these young men were good students, the brightest in the class. James was younger than David, but he was very large, with a sharp wit and tongue. Sam Jones was not related to David, but he certainly was a godsend. Sam had grown up in a Welsh home, and though he had spoken English as a boy, he understood Welsh. He read daily from his Welsh Bible and therefore was of immeasurable help to David, who was having a struggle adapting to English as his primary language. David understood English fairly well, having heard it from neighbors, visiting preachers, and some of his relatives from Philadelphia; but now he was thrust into an intense study of many perplexing words and idioms. Sam helped him daily with his diction and translations, as David accepted the language handicap and pushed himself even harder to keep up with the others. In a few short months, the other boys had almost forgotten that David's slight accent indicated anything unique about his ability to do the required work.

John Davis, Hezekiah Smith, David Thomas, Isaac Skillman, and Will Williams completed the class of eight. There were three classes at Hopewell Baptist Academy, also called "Isaac Eaton's Latin Grammar School" by some of the residents. The classes were divided by age, David's group being the oldest. Most of the students were residents of the Hopewell area and rode to classes daily from their homes. Those young men paid tuition for their instruction, but the others, like David, paid for their room, board, and instruction by doing household and farm chores for the Eatons. Horses, cattle, sheep, a few pigs, and several acres of feed grain had to be cared for by the boys in order to insure that the small farm could maintain enough food for the twenty-five to thirty people who ate there daily. David and eleven others lived in a separate house behind the Eatons' residence.

The Hopewell Academy was the first distinctively Baptist training school in America. Rev. Isaac Eaton came to Hopewell Baptist Church as pastor in 1748 from Southampton, Pennsylvania. There was a school in Hopewell at the time called the "Golden School-house" where Isaac taught the younger children of the community, but the Golden Schoolhouse provided only a general education for youngsters of all religious persuasions. At the same time, a great need was mounting for Baptist ministers in the colonies. Compared to the Congregationalists, Anglicans, and Quakers, Baptists were a small, though expanding, minority. Without schools to train their ministers, the few new churches that were being organized were destitute of qualified leadership. The Philadelphia Association of Baptists had issued a plea for ministers in 1732 by calling for a day of fasting and prayer, that God would "call" men to the ministry. The response brought forth many without either training or experience.

Isaac Eaton was distressed that Baptists were being maligned as ignorant and unworthy of respect in various communities. Some churches met only once per month and were led by uneducated, itinerant, part-time pastors. They were promptly dubbed "Thirty Day Baptists" in derision. Mr. Eaton had a deep conviction that God's call alone was not sufficient for a pastor to feed his people rich spiritual food. Therefore, in 1756, he began his first classes at Hopewell to train competent men to shepherd their Christian flocks. The church was strong, much larger than the small town of Hopewell suggested in 1756, and therefore many families entrusted their young men to Eaton's care for ministerial preparation. They were in capable hands.

Summer soon passed into early autumn, and the garden had long since ceased to produce vegetables when David decided to visit his cousin Abel Morgan in Middletown, New Jersey. David was sensitive to his responsibilities at the Academy, but he was anxious to get away for a few days. He had a restless spirit and abounding energy, enabling him to study long, profitable hours and then yearn for some physical exertion. He enjoyed riding his horse through the hill country to the west of Hopewell, but this autumn of 1758 he had a nagging desire to get away for a while. The weather had been clear for several days, displaying the beautiful, varying hues of the New Jersey trees and shrubs, and so David asked for and received permission from the Reverend Mr. Eaton to be gone for several days over a weekend. Ike Skillman was persuaded to accompany David on the forty-five mile trip with promises of good food and good friends, particularly the lovely young ladies of Middletown.

The boys were in no hurry as they left on Friday morning; so they decided to spend a night at Half-Way Inn on the New York-Philadelphia road. They arrived in good spirits at Cousin Abel's house in midafternoon on Saturday. Following unpacking, a hot bath, and a delicious meal served by bachelor Abel's mother, the three men settled down in the study for discussions of the Hopewell school, Baptist churches, and several topics of theology. A hopeful expectation of Abel's capable preaching the next day was on Ike's mind as they retired for the night. David's thoughts were on a Middletown family named Stillwell and their twin daughters.

The next day, David stood beside Abel and Ike as the pastor greeted the incoming members of the church.

"You're David Jones from Delaware, aren't you?" The question was asked by a lovely sixteen-year-old girl with a bright blue ribbon tied around her Sunday hat.

"Well, yes, I am, but I'm in school at Hopewell now," he replied. The remainder of the family, including the identical twin to the girl in blue ribbons, joined the girl and the three men.

"Good morning, Preacher!" Joseph Stillwell was a portly man with a quick smile and a hearty handshake. In addition to being the chairman of the elders and deacons of the church, he was acknowledged as the leader of the community. He wrote the town records, and few problems in the area were solved without first consulting Deacon Stillwell. He also owned one of the richest farms in the entire region.

"Good morning, Brother Stillwell. I'd like you to meet Isaac Skillman, and I believe you may remember David Jones, my cousin from Welsh Tract?"

"Why, yes, I do remember. It's a pleasure to see you again. I'm happy to make your acquaintance, Mr. Skillman. What brings you men to Middletown?" He looked at David as he spoke, but David was sharing a brief smile with the twin wearing red ribbons.

"Oh, ahh, we are just visiting Cousin Abel and having a break from our studies at Hopewell Academy," he said, directing his attention to Mr. Stillwell.

"You're some of Reverend Eaton's 'Young Parsons' then? How is the Reverend? All right, I hope?"

David and Ike nodded simultaneously.

"David, why don't you introduce Mr. Skillman to my daughters? You remember Mary and Ann, don't you?"

"Yes, sir. Of course I remember them. Ike, I mean Isaac; this is Ann and Mary Stillwell. Ann, Mary, this is Isaac Skillman from Pennsylvania."

David felt a nervousness that was uncharacteristic. He wasn't able to concentrate on the conversation and the girls at the same time; so he turned away from the ladies and listened as Abel and Mr. Stillwell talked. Throughout the service, and afterward, David was aware of the presence of the girls in the Stillwell pew. As the Stillwells departed, the father approached David.

"It has been nice seeing you again, David. I just told Pastor Morgan that the next time you come over, we would have all of you Welshmen over for Sunday dinner; that is, if you promise not to speak that gutteral Welsh! I want to hear about Pastor Davis, your mother and father, and all about the Academy."

David thanked him and vowed to himself that he just might make such an arrangement quite soon. He waved good-bye to Mrs. Stillwell and the girls waiting in the carriage.

The Thanksgiving and Christmas seasons came quickly, and the Academy students departed for their homes to enjoy the festive holiday activities. David was especially happy to be home, for neither his father nor his mother was well. Thankfully, the other Jones boys had worked and gathered a good crop in spite of their father's illness. All the family was present, though, and somehow they all felt especially close, as much love was expressed and felt.

The study of languages at Hopewell came easily for David. That interest and his desire to visit Middletown and the Stillwells again fused a plan of action in his mind. It was an acknowledged fact among the educated Christians in the middle colonies that Abel Morgan was the foremost Greek scholar of the area. Abel always welcomed giving David helpful points with that language, and of course there was that invitation from Mr. Stillwell. It didn't require much persuasion on David's part to convince the Reverend Mr. Eaton that he should go.

Ike Skillman made it very obvious to David that he would be pleased to receive another invitation to go, but no such invitation was forthcoming. David envisioned himself as the recipient of personal Greek instruction from Abel and of personal attention from the Stillwell girls. Ike was visibly miffed as David rode off in late February, but David smiled and felt quite pleased that he had a plan that just might afford him a very good time. He was not to be disappointed.

Kings Highway leads travelers from the west into Middletown past the Anglican, Baptist, and Methodist churches. The roadway follows the contour of Barclay Hill down to the junction of the New York road. There, the village of Middletown is surrounded by numerous farms, forming what looked like a large checkerboard of rectangular orchards and ploughed fields. One of the largest orchards surrounded one of the loveliest houses in that section of the colony, the home of Joseph Stillwell. David rode in the backseat of Abel's carriage as he accompanied Abel and his mother down the hill in response to an invitation to dine with the Stillwells.

A servant greeted the carriage as they rode up the lane between tall, barren elm trees. David saw that several figures were watching out two large windows on each side of the door as they approached. It was not difficult to see bright red and blue ribbons bobbing up and down behind the long cotton curtains as the girls jostled for a better view. Mr. Stillwell greeted the men warmly as his family stood behind him. David greeted Mrs. Stillwell—a short, heavy-set, and reserved woman. Next to her was her daughter, twenty-four-year-old Sarah, and her husband, John Cox. John, the oldest Stillwell son, was twenty-two years old, and he shook hands warmly with David. Catherine, nineteen, was next, followed by one of the twins in blue ribbons. Elizabeth, thirteen, nine-year-old Daniel, and seven-year-old Joseph were next in line. At the end of the line, by her own choosing, stood Ann, dressed in a lovely beige wool dress trimmed with red ribbons.

As they were seated in the parlor, John spoke to David. "How did you learn to tell the twins apart? We can't always distinguish them."

"Oh, I remember their ribbons," answered David.

"David," Mr. Stillwell spoke in a laughing voice, "I'm sure the girls would rather you had remembered their intelligent personalities than their ribbons." He laughed just a bit immoderately. John joined his father in laughter as David looked at a spot on the carpet.

Abel and Mrs. Morgan smiled, and the girls blushed. Ann darted a quick, piqued look at her father.

As they were seated at the table later, Mr. Stillwell continued to capitalize on the twins' embarrassment.

"You know," he said with twinkling eyes, "perhaps the reason Mary and Ann are so much alike is that when they were little, their mother used to put them in a big hogshead with the lid on when they were naughty. They would squeal and cry for a while in that big barrel, and when she pulled them out, their hair and dresses were so mussed up, you couldn't tell them apart. You never knew whether they were fighting one another or the hogshead to get out!" He laughed heartily at his little family disclosure.

"Oh, Sarah, that's cruel!" said Mrs. Morgan.

"It didn't hurt them any," said Mrs. Stillwell, "and besides, I got a lot done while they were put away."

David was appalled. Later, in the parlor, he asked John if Mrs. Stillwell really had put the twins in the hogshead.

"Put the twins in?" he laughed. "She has put us all in there at one time or another."

David frowned as he looked at John.

"Oh, she's right, you know," said John. "If you discipline children hard enough, you don't have to do it often. Besides, I didn't stay in the old barrel long before I knew it was better to be good than it was to be in that dark place. I can remember the twins, though, fighting like two cats over a clothesline." He laughed at the image of Mary and Ann completely filling the barrel and shrieking.

"Well, I'll admit that it doesn't seem to have hurt them any," said David, as he watched the girls serving tea across the room. John followed David's gaze and anticipated his wishes.

"Come on, David. Let's go talk to them. Which color ribbon do you prefer?" He smiled a knowing smile.

David returned the smile, looked back at the girls serving on each side of the table, and tried to be casual as he answered, "Oh, red, I guess."

The Stillwells provided a fine day for David. Mr. Stillwell was a big, friendly man described by his neighbors as a "very good man with a very large paunch." Mrs. Stillwell was uneducated, but hardworking and a strict disciplinarian. Though she could neither read nor write, she conducted an efficient house and farm.

To non-family members, the twins were identical. Even those in the immediate family were not always sure of their identity, and it was not unusual for the girls to fool their parents and brothers and sisters by switching ribbons. Since the family did not appreciate such antics, they insisted on the wearing of the proper ribbons at all times, red for Ann and blue for Mary. The girls were of medium height and frame, and strikingly pretty. Poor older sister Catherine tried hard to keep up with her lively twin sisters, but both in physical attractiveness and vibrant personality she was unequal to the task. As they matured, Mary and Ann enjoyed traveling, laughing, reading, and friends. The only people who had reservations about them were the other young ladies of Middletown who competed for the attentions of young men.

David was attracted to Ann. He had found ways to visit with her in those special, private ways in the midst of groups at home and church. In September, the annual meeting of the Philadelphia Baptist Association met in Hopewell. It was the desire of most of the churches to meet there in order to view the progress of the Academy, as well as to conduct Association business. With David's urging, Ann convinced her father that she and Mary could and should help represent their church at the meeting. Their brother John was David's age, and the two young men developed a deep friendship. John sensed David's desire to be with Ann, and he therefore arranged for the twins to be with him as he visited with David. At the Association meeting to which they all came, there was ample opportunity for them to be together at public meetings and in private conversations. It was a comfortable arrangement for Ann and David as they slowly and surely grew to appreciate and desire one another's company.

In November, David received an urgent message from his mother at Welsh Tract: "Come home. Your father is dying." The Jones family gathered at the farm and watched helplessly as Morgan Jones lost strength, weight, and even the will to live. He died with his children by his bedside on December 6, 1759.

Two days after the funeral, several of the brothers were helping with the chores when a rider approached. The boys continued to work as John went to the house to assist his mother. In a few minutes, the rider left and John approached the group with a paper in his hand. He smiled at David.

"Well, Davey boy. I do declare that this here letter with your name on it smells like lilac. Now where do you suppose they grow flowers in December? Middletown, New Jersey?" He pushed the letter behind him as David reached out his hand.

"Give it to me, John."

"I sure don't remember Momma Morgan's perfume smelling like this, Davey boy." The other boys had stopped working as they stood watching with big grins spread across their faces.

"Give it to me, John. I don't think this is respectful to Pa to carry on like this." He wasn't smiling.

David snatched the letter away as it was offered and stomped toward the clump of trees by the edge of the field. He didn't appreciate levity at a time when he grieved over his father and when he desperately hoped that the handwriting might be Ann's. He carefully tore the edges of the single sheet of folded paper and ran his eyes swiftly over the words. It was from Ann. She had heard of Mr. Jones' illness. She was praying for him. Would David write her about his father? Would he be coming to Middletown again soon? He ran his eyes to the conclusion. It was signed rather formally: "Ann Stillwell, Middletown, New Jersey."

The last months of winter and the first months of spring found David studying harder than ever. His environment was pleasant; his studies were challenging; and he was financially secure with the small inheritance that had come with the settlement of his father's will. Still, he went about his duties with intensity, as if he were preparing for some impending struggle. At the time when life was pleasant for most twenty-four-year-old men, David pushed his mind and body hard. Time seemed short, and lost souls appeared imminently in his thinking. Never a stout boy, David had grown even more slender with the passing years. He was all bones and gristle, and his small bits of humor were suppressed behind a serious face. Occasionally he allowed a dry joke or a barbed thrust to escape his grave demeanor, but he held himself in check from a full expression of the kind, considerate nature that lay deep within him. He pursued Ann in that same determined, calculated manner.

He visited Middletown once more in the spring. During that visit, he talked seriously with Abel about the Morgans' previous invitation to spend the summer with them. Abel urged him to come for several reasons. He truly needed some work done on the parsonage, and there was the garden to tend. Abel laughed when he observed David's expression at the mention of "garden." They could study Greek and have nearly three months to talk theology together.

Then, too, Abel was eager for David to follow his ministerial routine and observe the duties of a minister at firsthand. No mention of Ann was made, but both men understood that David spoke more and more of the Stillwells and of Ann. Abel approved, but he refrained from interfering with the initiative David was taking. Ann appeared pleased with the idea of David's coming for the summer; so David made his plans accordingly.

The summer was most pleasant for David, for he was particularly pleased with studying only when he desired and choosing what he wanted to study. Abel was a considerate and intelligent teacher. There was no pressure; therefore David set his own pace. He had many occasions to see Ann, dropping by to see her, seeing her on Sundays; and once Ann surprised him with a visit.

David and Abel were in the Morgan parlor translating a difficult passage of Scripture from the Greek when they heard a knock at the door. Abel opened the door to see two lovely young ladies dressed in the bright popular sacques of the day. Each wore canary silk dresses hanging from the shoulders over a slightly hooped petticoat. Neither wore lace or sashes, but each had her distinctive band of ribbon loosely tied around her small bonnet. Ann held a basket covered with a blue-and-white-checkered linen cloth.

"Mary! Ann! What a beautiful sight! Come in out of that hot sun."

"We knew you were studying. John told us. So we brought you some cakes and tea if you want them," said Ann, looking first at Abel and then at David, who had come to the door by then.

"Why, of course we would be delighted to be served by such thoughtful young ladies," said Abel.

The girls began busying themselves clearing the rectangular dinner table of lexicons, grammars, and Bibles. David hadn't spoken as yet, and even though he was quite surprised to see them, he was extremely pleased. The girls served the small cakes on plates and then handed them teacups and napkins. Abel pulled four chairs into a circle and indicated that they should be seated.

"Well, now, to what do we owe the honor of this visit?" said Abel.

The girls glanced at each other and Mary spoke with a sly grin, "Well, you see, we agreed to tell you that we made the cakes so you two would be impressed, but here in the house of a 'reverend' we can't tell a lie. So the truth is, Mum made them, and we wanted an excuse for a ride and some nice company."

Abel laughed heartily at her candid honesty, and David grinned as he enjoyed the refreshments. David still hadn't spoken. In a few moments, Mary took another sip of her tea, as Abel sat up alertly and spoke to her, "Mary, I want to send you girls home with some apples. How would you like to help me?"

Mary stood up quickly and said, "You know, Reverend Morgan, that's really the third reason we came."

Ann smiled and shook her head slowly as the others burst into laughter. When they left, David spoke warmly, "Thank you so much for coming, Ann. You're very thoughtful."

"It's our pleasure, I assure you. You might even enjoy all this more if you knew how we plotted to get Mum to do this so we could get out of the house. You would have thought we were two spies in an enemy camp, but it surely did work." She burst into giggles as she added, "And you should have seen Catherine frown at us from the kitchen sink as we left."

David wanted to introduce a more personal thought, but he could not force himself into seriousness on this day. The conversation turned to lighthearted topics, and they soon joined Mary and Abel in the orchard. It had been an unexpected and very pleasant surprise, a satisfying experience in which much effort had been expended to get David alone with Ann.

Twice during the summer months, David was called home due to the protracted illness of his mother. She was bedridden from early summer until September when she died quietly in her sleep. David was still in Middletown when the news came from Welsh Tract. As he packed his saddlebags for a fast ride south, Ann and her brother John arrived at the Morgans. Abel visited with John, who remained in the carriage as Ann approached David standing by his horse. Her eyes glistened with tears. She held a piece of folded paper and a small sack in her hand.

"Oh, David, I'm terribly sorry for your loss. You've been through so much suffering lately. I wrote something for you, but would you not read it until after you get to Delaware? Please let us hear from you soon."

David took the sack and paper and said, "Thank you, Ann. I'll be returning to Hopewell from the Tract, you know, but I'll write."

"Please be careful. I don't know how I could stand what you have endured these past months with your father and now your mother and all."

David shrugged his shoulders and shook his head in a gesture that said that he didn't know, either. He wanted to say something more, to reach out and touch her in an expression of thankfulness and tenderness. Abel and John weren't watching them. He looked at Ann and then slowly lowered his head.

"Good-bye, Ann."

"God be with you and yours, David."

She turned very slowly with throbbing head and aching heart. David felt a huge lump in his throat that prohibited his uttering a sound in spite of his desire to call her back. Ann continued walking away.

He resumed his studies at Hopewell following the funeral. On November 20, a rider arrived in Hopewell from Middletown with more sad news for David. Joseph Stillwell had been hastening into town when a neighbor saw him clutch his chest and fall from his horse. He was dead before anyone reached him. The funeral had been a week ago. David's jaw set in a grim, hard line at the news. "Oh, Annie!" he muttered softly. Without a further word he started for his room and then to the pasture for his horse. Riding all night, he arrived at Abel's house at daybreak. He freshened, changed his clothes, and rode with Abel to the Stillwells. He was relieved to find Ann composed, though deeply saddened. He returned to Hopewell before the week was over, though he couldn't ever remember leaving with such sadness before.

Perhaps it was the loss of both of his parents within ten months, or perhaps it was that sad visit with Ann in November that made David restless and irritable. Or was it the longing to see Ann, combined with the beautiful spring of 1761, that accounted for his loss of concentration on his studies? Mr. Eaton finally called David aside for a personal conference in an attempt to determine what was troubling the young man. He closed the conversation with an astute suggestion.

"David," he said, "I want you to do something. Without going into detail, I want you to visit Reverend Morgan for a while. He will be happy to have you, and I think you need to get away. The garden is in, your studies are progressing nicely, and so I really want you to go." His countenance indicated that he meant exactly what he said. David wrote both Abel and Ann, and in March he left for Middletown. He lived with his cousin Abel, of course, and his presence in the parsonage and in the church were assets as he helped with chores at the Morgans, aided in the repair of the church, and continued his studies in Greek and theology.

As he found some time for himself, he slept long hours and often went riding alone. One day he rode to the coast overlooking Sandy Hook. His was a restive spirit; he was a man with a thwarted purpose. Normally outspoken, he now had a message that somehow couldn't be delivered. Ann was the problem, to be sure. He confided in no one, but everyone knew. He had asked Ann on the previous Thursday to spend a day with him riding in the hills, but she hesitated. She would think about it. Then she was gone north over the weekend to visit relatives as David agonized over how to communicate his true feelings to her. On her return, however, she did agree to a picnic. David was cautiously optimistic.

The day was clear and warm. They began to eat the covered dishes of food without enthusiasm. David was so preoccupied with expressing himself to Ann that his usual hearty appetite deserted him. He ate, but his eyes and interest were on Ann. Ann, too, was not really hungry. Seldom did she eat much, and now here in the beautiful woods, the excitement of being with David on a special occasion quenched whatever appetite she might have had.

"Ann, I want you to know that I am enjoying myself. I'm very happy that you came with me. The food is good, it's a beautiful day, and I'm just, well, just happy."

"I am, too, David," she said.

"Ann, this means a great deal to me that you agreed to come." His voice was more serious now.

"I know," she said.

"You almost didn't come, I know, and maybe it's too early for us to be out here, but we have known each other a long time."

"I'm glad it worked out, David."

David put down his piece of fried fish, looked straight into Ann's eyes and said, "Ann, there are so many things that have been on my mind when I am with you; and when I am away from you, I think of you more often than I probably should with my studies and all. I've wanted so often just to say, 'Ann, let's take a walk; let's talk a while; let me share some things I've been thinking and studying.' I've wished you could read over my sermons before I go to Freehold to preach, and, well, there are just other things that I want to say." He paused.

Ann placed her food on the napkin, carefully wiped her fingers, caught David's gaze, and held it transfixed. Speaking very carefully, she replied, "And, David, I want to hear it all."

David's mind went blank. His tongue refused to move. *Could it be,* he thought, *that she feels as I do? Is that an opening for me to proceed? Surely not. Why should she feel anything for me?* It seemed that an eternity passed while David's mind raced like a wild pony. Instinctively, he pushed his food away. There was no further thought of food or eating or anything but Ann. David was the first to lower his eyes and break the silence.

"I'm not hungry anymore," he said with lowered voice. He hated the words as soon as they were uttered. His heart wanted to say so much more, but his mind had gone blank. His comment about not being hungry made him feel like a fool.

"I'm not either," she whispered in a barely audible voice. She, too, now lowered her head and stared at some unseen object on the cloth. David knew he must break the silence. He desperately wanted to touch her hand, to speak words of love, to hold her, but his nervousness precluded rational expressions at the moment. The silence was deafening. He knew he had to do something, for this was that special moment between them. All his preconceived speeches, however, were far too jumbled to make sense out of them now. He shifted nervously.

"Why don't we take a ride?" he asked.

"Fine, David," Ann replied.

They packed the food and folded the cloth in silence. Walking down the small rise of land to the buggy, David felt an urge to reach out in a gesture of physical support and intimacy and grasp Ann's arm as she walked. But he couldn't.

What is the matter with me? The thought thundered through his brain. *Why can't I take that one step of expression? But then, why should I? She and Mary have been entertaining other young men. I am only a preacher, and one without a church at that. If she rebuffed me, I think I would die. If she turned away from me, well, I just couldn't stand it. I could never face her again, or her family. She deserves more than a person like me. I simply cannot, I will not, risk her refusal of my love. No, I just can't.*

"It's a beautiful afternoon," Ann broke the silence, for she sensed a struggle within her companion.

Easily now, the conversation turned toward the things they loved and felt comfortable with. Sharing their rich heritage together, recounting their recent losses, laughing at their relations with brothers and sisters, they drove on happily.

"Say, Ann, what do you say to an ice-cold drink on this warm, spring afternoon?"

"Well, fine, David, but our bottles of water are lukewarm by now."

"Oh, no, I don't mean that. I mean the ice down by the spring near the Wickersham place."

"You know, David, I've never been over there. John and Thomas have always ridden over there to get our ice for us in the summer."

"Good," said David as he flicked the reins and the horse picked up his gait. "It's time you saw it."

He determined that, as they walked back to the ice, he would say something to express his love to Ann. He would take her hand. He would tell her he loved her. He would hold her. Yes, he would this time. His nervousness mounted as they neared the ice buried in the north side of the hill. Several nearby farmers cut ice from the streams and ponds in late winter and placed it in a deep ravine by the spring. They packed it with sawdust, and then on special occasions when company came in the summer, they came to chip some away for cold drinks.

The path down the hill was covered with overhanging branches, almost hiding the sun's rays. There was moss on both sides of the path, and it was cool and pleasant. David's anxiety mounted as he walked slightly behind Ann while they worked their way to the spring. This was a perfect spot to be with the woman you love, or think you love. Yes, this was a better place to express himself than at the picnic lunch. As they stood there, he would slip his hand into hers, tell her he loved her, and hope and pray that she would respond positively.

"Why, Ann! What are you doing here?" asked Jim Marshall, a young family friend of the Stillwells who was chipping ice as they turned down the path that ended at the spring. If he had been surprised by a savage Indian, David couldn't have been any more startled, angered, or frustrated. He controlled his words, but his face turned into a slow scowl, and his stomach knotted in sick frustration.

"Oh, Jimmy! You startled me!" said Ann. "We just came by for an ice drink, that's all." There was a strained pause. "Jimmy, have you met David Jones? He's from Delaware, and he's studying here with Pastor Morgan."

"Well, we haven't met, but I've heard about you. Nice to meet you, David."

Jim tried to shake hands with David across the spring, but it was too far to reach. All of them felt awkward. The size of Jim's icebuckets indicated to David that it was going to be a long time before he was through; so he accepted the offered ice chips, drank a glass of water with Ann, and then the two of them went on their way.

David was out of ideas now. Every effort to speak of his true feelings to Ann had been squelched by his own timidity or unfortunate timing. He felt a deep desire to close out the whole world in a pall of heavy silence. His thoughts and emotions turned inward, and he struggled to be pleasant with Ann and with himself. He desperately wished he could be alone. He had failed, and he desired to torture himself with every intimate detail of his miserable attempts at romance. They rode over the winding road in silence for a few minutes as they headed for home. Conversation returned, but it was forced and unnatural, for there was an invisible barrier between them. There was something that needed to be said. Feelings crying out for expression were torturing David. If only he knew what was in Ann's mind! Could she know of his torment, his frustration? Couldn't she say something?

David caught a fleeting glimpse of the valley as they bounced along the hilly road. He knew they would soon be home, and he couldn't go on, not yet.

"Do you mind if we drive just a bit more before we go home, Ann?" he asked as he turned very calmly and looked deeply into her eyes.

"I'd love to, David," she answered softly as she caught his eye and held it.

They turned off on a rough new road only recently cut through the woods to some new houses. They both smiled at the bumpiness of the crude wagon path, and David wisely turned the carriage around. Just before reaching the main road again, he noticed a break in the trees and reined the horse up so that they looked out on the beautiful valley below. It was late afternoon, now, and the sun's soft yellow fingers touched the outskirts of Middletown with its warm rays.

"It's beautiful, isn't it?" said Ann as she looked toward her family land. "Is it this lovely in Delaware, David?"

"Ann!" David spoke with a quiet urgency. She turned quickly and saw that he had been looking at her, not the scenery. He lowered his head and fought for words. Ann turned sideways to the carriage and placed her arm on the back of the seat pointing toward David. He looked up and placed his right hand on her arm. He began to speak, but the words were jumbled without real meaning, almost incoherent. Neither of them would be able to recall exactly what was said next.

"Ann, I would never want to say or do anything that would displease you. I mean, I want you to understand what I feel . . . that is, I hope you know that you mean something special, very close . . . I wouldn't want to hurt you or make you feel uncomfortable. . . ."

He paused and knew this was not the time for further bumbling words. Ann's expression did not change. David slid across the seat and took her in his arms. He kissed her firmly, fully on her lips. She responded with a warmth beyond his greatest hope. For those few brief moments, time stood still. Her fragrance, her touch, her response melted into his very being. It was as if he had held and loved her forever before this moment. It was a strange, yet familiar, feeling that engulfed him. He had expected this time of physical embrace to be awkward and full of well-expressed words more than real physical contact, but David felt deep meaning flowing from his heart to hers as he held her close. He should have felt embarrassed, he thought later, but he experienced only relief at her response. Later, he was almost shocked at his next words as he gently pushed himself away from her, held her at arm's length, and spoke softly and fervently in emotion-choked Welsh:

"R wyn dy garu, Anniefach" ("I love you, little Annie"). He pulled her back to him again and kissed her lightly on the cheek. She understood that Welsh expression quite well, but his expression had said it long before the words were uttered. She waited a brief moment and then gently pushed herself to arm's length. Her eyes welled with glistening tears of happiness. She spoke softly, slowly, for fear a longer breath would feed a sob.

"Oh, David, and I love you, too!"

She reached out to him now, and as she kissed him, the small trickle of tears turned to a fountain of joyful weeping.

The family was delighted to give their permission for the engagement of David and Ann. The marriage, it was agreed by all, would come whenever David concluded his studies and settled into a pastorate. His educational program at Hopewell had originally been planned as a four-year course, similar to that of the existing colleges. However, David was older than the usual student; thus he began to develop another plan.

Middletown Baptist Church had been sponsoring a group from their community which had moved into the Freehold area. Those Baptists had erected a meetinghouse near Crosswicks Creek in an area called Upper Freehold, and though they met more than once per month, they could not as yet afford to support a minister. The Middletown congregation accepted the responsibility of supplying a preacher for each service, and in addition to Pastor Morgan's occasional visits, David was frequently asked to speak. The Welsh Tract church, as was customary for one's home congregation, had licensed David to preach in the summer of 1761. Crosswicks enjoyed David's preaching, for he was positive, straightforward, fully indoctrinated, and he came with the blessing of Abel Morgan. In time, he was asked to preach at Crosswicks at least once each month.

To complete his education, David came back to Middletown in the fall of 1761 to study with Abel. In that way, he could continue his studies, have a place to gain the experience of preaching, and be nearer to Ann at the same time. It was a delightful experience for all concerned. In good weather, Ann, with Mary and Mrs. Stillwell, often accompanied David to his preaching duties.

The engaged couple had ample opportunity to be together, and on all but a few occasions they had a wonderful time. One exception was an August Sunday when David dined with the Stillwells following worship at Middletown.

After a sumptuous dinner in the family dining room, David suggested that Ann might enjoy a ride. She readily agreed and went to her room with Mary to change clothes. In a few minutes a lovely young lady appeared in a long-waisted bodice of beige, holding a matching wide-brimmed bonnet trimmed with red ribbon.

"My, but you look lovely, Annie," he said as she approached the carriage.

She smiled.

He held her arm as she stepped up and took her seat. He patted her affectionately on the arm as he turned to go around and sit beside her. Oddly, he thought he heard an unusual coughing sound as he moved away.

"Where would you like to go?" he asked, as they moved down the lane toward the road.

"Oh, anywhere is fine. Wherever you choose, David," she spoke as she turned away from him.

He spoke in an animated voice after a pause. "Annie, would you rather be married in the summer than the winter or fall?"

The response was a coughing-laughing sound. He turned sharply toward her.

"What's the matter?" he said, startled.

"Oh, nothing," she said lightly. "I just have a cough."

He stared at her searchingly. He turned his head slowly to the front, but something bothered him. He tried to put it out of his mind.

"Well, talk to me about your latest ideas concerning our wedding."

She giggled.

He snapped his head toward her and his expression was not pleasant.

"What in the world is the matter with you?"

She slid down in the seat, lowered her head, and laughed uncontrollably. There was a pause as he stared at her, and then David jerked hard on the reins. The horse reared up at the unexpected halt.

"Mary! I don't think this is funny!" He was hot with anger. He sat still for just a moment as he absorbed the full realization that Ann and her identical twin had tricked him by switching clothes and ribbons. He jumped down from the carriage and strode with long steps to the horse. Grasping the bit very roughly, he began leading, almost pulling, the horse, carriage, and Mary back to the house. Mary, in hysterical laughter now, covered her face and attempted to subdue the sounds of her merriment. David was in a rage as he stepped to the front porch where Ann, her mother, and several of her brothers and sisters had watched the entire proceeding. Since Ann was aware of David's anger, she attempted to suppress her laughter, but the huge grin on her face could not be concealed.

"I fail to see the humor in this, Ann. I made a fool out of myself with Mary just now."

"David!" Ann exclaimed in mock horror. "Whatever did you do and say to my sister?" John and Mrs. Stillwell roared with laughter as David clenched his fists. His face reddened.

"Don't you ever do this again!" His rising voice had the quiver of deep-seated anger. The laughter stopped as he turned on his heel and stalked past Mary to the barn and his horse. Ann felt immediately sorry that she had tricked and teased him. She felt pain now for his embarrassment, and she made her way toward him. Speaking softly, she calmed him and brought him back to the house, but not before David spoke to her quite sternly.

"I mean it, Ann. Don't ever do this again, and I don't ever want to hear of this whole affair ever again."

The close proximity of David and Ann in Middletown undoubtedly hastened their wedding day. So, too, did the fact that Crosswicks built a church parsonage and, with an ulterior motive in mind, invited David to come and live there, since he was now their "regular" preacher. The ulterior motive, of course, was that the small congregation had taken the young couple to their hearts and had desired to play the role of Cupid. They were successful, for Ann Stillwell became Mrs. David Jones on February 22, 1762. They moved into the parsonage, the beginning of forty-seven years of successful, if not continuously smooth, marriage.

In December, the happy couple was blessed with the birth of a daughter whom they named Eleanor in honor of David's mother. Since David's studies, the young family, and the church were all prospering, David pushed hard for Crosswicks to declare itself independent of the Middletown congregation. Older, wiser heads, however, desired a slower pace, wishing for financial income to match the physical increase of the congregation. David could not accept that reasoning.

In August, 1764, David persuaded an old friend in the Middletown church to request his ordination to the gospel ministry. Licensing of a minister was customarily granted in order to give a man the right to preach, but ordination was reserved for the day that licensed man became a full-time pastor. Only then could he administer the ordinances of the church. Baptist churches recognized two special rituals requiring the administration of a fully ordained minister, baptism and Communion. The act of setting a man apart as a fully ordained minister implied that such a person was mature and capable of counseling and preaching as well as directing the two special ordinances. David reasoned that though his church was only an extension of the Middletown group, he was still the full-time minister at Crosswicks. The Reverend Abel

Morgan counseled David to be patient for the fast-approaching time when Crosswicks would become an independent church. At the proper time, Middletown Baptist Church would recommend his ordination. David disagreed with his cousin and attempted to have certain of his friends vote his ordination over Pastor Morgan's objections.

At the business meeting in August, 1764, the two positions were presented. Obadiah Barclay spoke in David's behalf, and Samuel Bray for Pastor Morgan. David should have remained silent, but his enthusiastic nature burst forth with exclamations of his "rights" to ordination. His tone of voice, his choice of words, and his forceful manner solidified the church against him, though his intensity precluded his own recognition of that attitude. A motion to delay any decision received all but two votes: Mr. Barclay's and David's.

The issue should have been laid quietly to rest for a time, but David forced the question once more in December. Again, David rose to speak in the meeting and, with his face flushed in anger, began to plead his case. "It is the right of any licensed Baptist minister to be ordained when he is serving a church in a full-time manner. I demand to know why I should not be ordained. I should either be a preacher of the gospel or I should have charges brought against me that would prohibit me. In short, gentlemen, either ordain me or silence me."

Pastor Morgan spoke in a kind voice as he explained to David that Crosswicks was a part of the Middletown congregation and therefore not an autonomous church. When Crosswicks became an independent body, they could ordain whom they chose with Middletown's blessing. A vote on the issue followed, with a large majority voting against David's proposition.

Following the vote, David jumped to his feet and said: "I demand to know why I am not being ordained. Before this meeting, the majority of people were for me, except for a few who are prejudiced against me. I ask for another vote. Pastor Morgan has not quoted my words as I said them, and I think you would vote differently if you knew exactly what I said. No one has yet said why I am not being ordained. I demand to know."

James Mott immediately leaped to his feet, demanding a censure for the high-handed actions and accusations of young Jones. The meeting was in an uproar. Pastor Morgan held up his hand until order had been restored. Then he said: "David, you ask why we don't ordain you? Let me tell you. Your very action here tonight is the reason. Your lack of humility, your precipitous remarks, and most of all, your lack of prudence speak very clearly to the point that you are not ready to assume the role of a shepherd of God's sheep. I have the distinct feeling that when you are ready to discuss God's business quietly, rationally, and lovingly, then, and only then, some congregation will be more than pleased to ordain you." There was little left to say. The meeting dismissed quietly and quickly, and David rode home in sullen silence.

Whatever his shortcomings, David possessed a sincere desire and a strong personal discipline to become a good minister. Two years later, his hard work, faithful study, and a love of his people led to his ordination as the first pastor of the Crosswicks Baptist Church.

3

Restlessness and Conflict

Dr. Tallman watched David work in the small, poorly lighted room. Various bottles of liquid occupied the table with herbs, seeds, and books. A stack of papers was spread loosely on the table. The flicker of a small fire was barely visible in a tiny, portable cast-iron stove in the corner.

"Just follow the directions, David. One gallon of sound state cider with a double handful of parsley roots. Cut the tops fine. That's it. That's right."

David added two tablespoons of bruised mustard seed, one-half ounce ointment of squills, and one ounce of juniper berries.

"Now mix it slowly and thoroughly, and we'll keep it warm here by the fire for twenty-four hours."

The doctor hurried off to another room as David continued to read the directions for making a medicine that would cure the dropsy. "After twenty-four hours, shake the contents violently and drain off the rudiments on top. The dose for an adult is one-half wine glass three times per day when the stomach is mostly empty. When the water is discharged, the patient should use moderately." Satisfied that the formula was in good order, David set the large jar of liquid close to the fire, picked up the copy of John Tennent's book, *Every Man His Own Doctor,* leaned back in his chair, and began reading the paragraph titled "An Extra-Ordinary Eye Water."

Doctors Moore and Tallman of Bordentown, New Jersey, were the only trained physicians in the area between Philadelphia and New York, and because of the growing needs of isolated farm families, they had originated a plan for training other men to become doctors. David was one of those who desired to become a medical practitioner. Since his Crosswicks home was nearby, after his crops were harvested, he rode to Bordentown daily in the winter months for schooling. It was not unusual for ministers to practice medicine in his day as, oftentimes, they found the practice of medicine an effective means to supplement a meager pastoral salary. Then, too, ministers were sometimes the only educated people in rural areas, and farm families who had no experienced doctors to help them in times of serious injury and sickness turned to those who had even the barest of medical and surgical training. In the absence of more qualified persons, David had sometimes set broken bones, served home remedies, and bled sick and dying neighbors. Because of the high mortality rate, and realizing his inexperience in these important matters, David sought the education, training, and experience which only qualified doctors could give him.

The usual training program for a colonial doctor was attendance at a grammar school or academy, apprenticeship with an established doctor for two to four years, and then the organization of his own practice. Both Philadelphia and New York had medical schools by 1767, but the graduates were few in number and tended to practice their profession in the larger cities. The most prevalent medical problems of the day were influenza, smallpox, stomach disorders, and broken bones; these difficulties formed the basis of David's study.

There was another motivation, however, for David to study medicine. He and Ann had stood by the graveside of two of their children in those early years. David could not force from his mind the thought that those dear little ones might have survived if someone, anyone, nearby had been able to minister to their needs in those critical hours. Out there in a beautiful but lonely and isolated countryside, poor Ann would have had her spirit crushed had it not been for loving friends and a husband who determined to help others in similar circumstances by becoming a doctor. His strength surfaced in times of adversity, and his new exertion of will to combine medical study with farming and pastoring gave Ann a new source of hope and a will to live. David threw himself into his studies with a fury that Ann both admired and resented. He was gone from home quite often now, but it seemed to be for a good cause; so Ann accepted it with only a minimum of complaint.

David read about and experimented with medicines, such as Jesuit's bark, oil of cloves, seeds, laudanum, roots, and leaves of the many trees and bushes of the New Jersey countryside. Isolation and inoculation were observed as he accompanied the two doctors on

their rounds. He aided in the setting of broken limbs and was appalled to learn that 70 percent of all compound fractures resulted in death due to internal bleeding and infection. He observed that some medicines often left patients in a worse condition than before the arrival of doctors. Babies died at a high rate. The elderly suffered with stomach and bowel ailments. David was convinced that he could practice medicine better than those around him. His was a confidence in his own intelligence and ability coupled with a belief that God had called him to this work as he had called him to the ministry. More and more, David went out on his own to practice what he studied.

George Chafey was a member of David's church who lived ten miles to the east of Crosswicks. Mr. Chafey had been plagued with a hemorrhage of an old leg wound for several months and finally sent word by his family on Sunday that he wished for David to treat him. David read on the subject, packed several possible remedies in his saddlebags, and reached Mr. Chafey on Tuesday. Following an examination of the wound, David pulled a small bottle from his bag, removed the cork, and displayed a handful of greenish pills.

"Now, Mr. Chafey, I want you to take one of these each morning and one in the evening. You may feel weak and a bit giddy, maybe even nauseous. When this affects you, stop taking them for a while, and then repeat it."

"What's in these things, Reverend? They look like rotten peas to me."

David smiled and said, "Dr. Redman from Philadelphia has had fine success with these, Mr. Chafey, and I believe they will help you."

"Well, what's in them, anyway?"

"These are the leaves of spring hemlock. We pound them, squeeze out the juice, and expose them to the sun till they dry up like this." Most all the doctors in our region use them, and as I said, they have had exceptional success."

"You're sure?"

"I'm positive."

In two weeks, Mr. Chafey appeared at church with a beaming smile and an announcement that the "rotten peas" had cured him "sure as I'm standing here." David tried to hide his pleasure, yet had felt that it would turn out that way, since he had almost willed it to be so. The next Sunday, David presented Mr. Chafey with a bill of three dollars for the personal visit, medicine, and "professional advice."

George Chafey was stunned at the receipt of a bill from his pastor and, after a moment of hesitation, exploded in a torrent of heated words, "I'll not pay my pastor for services rendered. I helped pay for this church, and I help pay your salary." His words began pouring forth faster than ever now: "I've been generous with my money to every preacher who has preached here, but I will not start paying one to come see me. I've never paid for any other preacher to come see me, and I'll not start paying some young would-be Welsh preacher who thinks he's a doctor."

With that, he stalked off to the family buggy and left David with red face and mounting anger. Ann patted him lightly on the arm to calm him. Later in the week, a rider left a folded note from Mr. Chafey at the parsonage. The same vitriolic condemnation was repeated in the note, and then the message concluded by stating: "Your actions, Rev. Jones, contrast quite unfavorably with the conduct of Jesus. He healed the sick gratis. Is the servant better than the Master?" Mr. Chafey and other families of English heritage in the church thereafter referred to David's mixing of clergy and medicine as the "angelic connection." Their humor was barbed, but they were careful not to say it in the presence of this stern young man whose face could turn red in the presence of unhappy disagreement. David thereafter confined his medical practice to nonmembers or only to those close friends within the church who offered to pay as a part of their request for his services.

In 1770, New Jersey physicians promoted an examination for all new men who had studied to be doctors and who wished to practice in the state. David had had the necessary schooling and internship, but he resented being forced to study in preparation for extensive testing. His practice was small and he did not desire to be a full-time physician, he reasoned; so he found his interests turning increasingly away from medicine and toward other matters. Before 1772, when the physician's examination became law, David focused on an issue that would consume him for most of his life: ministering to the spiritual needs of Indians.

David was an adventurer at heart, a strange combination of one who studied long months with great intensity and then engaged in some new physical endeavor. He longed for rigorous exercise in nature's great wilderness, and no one ever knew him to postpone the opportunity to commune with his God on horseback while passing through the forest and over the streams and hills. His choice of a life of challenge and difficulty contrasted sharply with the lives of many of those around him who opted for the more secure, serene life of a settled country pastorate. Yet David could not be happy for long in a role of ease and calm stability. His church was a small congregation whose members put few requirements on their pastor. Still, a few members had withdrawn from the fellowship because of David's criticism of the mother country's demands on colonial assemblies, and besides, he was simply restless. He had learned all he desired to know of medicine and surgery, and so his eyes turned westward to the wilderness and the Indians.

It was impossible for a colonial pastor in 1772 to be oblivious to the native Americans all around him. Various religious societies had encouraged churches to preach the gospel of Christ to the Indians from the first founding of the colonies. Though Baptists were a small minority in 1772, and far too small to mount a cooperative effort in extensive missionary effort, David sought to be a pioneer in demonstrating to his fellow Baptists that preaching to Indians was a needed and worthy effort. He wrote on the day he departed for the Ohio River Valley that he hoped "to excite a pious emulation in some few better qualified to engage in the important work of civilizing the poor neglected heathen."

Ann watched the children say good-bye to their father in May, 1772. David's horse was saddled and tied to the big budding oak tree in front of the house as Ann fought back tears while holding little Morgan in her arms. Nine-year-old Eleanor held her brother Joseph's hand. He sobbed softly when his daddy hugged him.

"Now, you children be good and help your mother while I'm gone. I'll bring you some pretty presents from the Indians."

He turned toward Ann and Morgan. "Don't worry, Annie, Mr. Springer will take good care of the place, and if any of you need anything, the church people will be near. So don't worry, Annie."

"Oh, David!" Ann's tears flowed as he bent to kiss Morgan's soft cheek.

"Now, Ann, you know we are here to do our best to serve God as a minister and family. Everything will be all right."

He kissed her quickly and mounted his horse. He rode around the cemetery and cornfield, waving to the family group standing between the parsonage and church.

He wrote a diary in the form of a travelogue with every major stream, road, farmhouse, and inn noted. John Holmes, seeking to better his health by traveling, joined him near Philadelphia. In early May, they arrived at Fort Pitt, where they joined a party of surveyors and hunters led by George Rogers Clark. As they pointed their canoes downriver, David was exhilarated with the prospect of viewing the western wilderness firsthand and experiencing new and exciting adventures.

The excitement was little more than slow, difficult travel at first, and efforts at preaching to the few Indians encountered along the way proved frustrating. The hunters in the party were sarcastic, if not openly hostile, to the idea of preaching when so many miles needed to be covered to reach the skins and hides they desired. The language barrier also hindered the enthusiastic preacher, but he managed to condense his sermons into four succinct thoughts: (1) the state in which God created man, (2) man's fall into sin, (3) the promise of a Savior, and (4) the work of God in renewing souls to qualify them for heaven. He found that the Indians wished to learn to read, but expressed little desire to live better. A Shawnee chief, Yellow Hawk, told David that white men ought to leave Indian customs such as religion to the Indians.

Perhaps it was the intense heat of summer, or the marshy lowlands infested with huge mosquitoes, or perhaps it was the ill-prepared food which he ate that caused David to grow weak and suffer a high fever. David never appeared to be healthy. His body was so thin as to be described as frail by more than one person. He had suffered attacks of asthma in his youth, and now that old enemy returned in full fury. At last, the men in his party left him in a trapper's tent for fear that further travel and exposure would end his life in a harsh and humid wilderness. He lay for days in a hot, feverish sweat with the trapper's Indian wife and half-breed son his only hope of survival. Bitter herbal medicines were poured down his weakened body, and at last a long, deep sleep ensued. When he awoke, the fever was broken. He was extremely weak, but he would live.

The sun lay low on the horizon as David heard a cacophony of the sounds of a dispute outside the tent. The heat had dissipated somewhat, and he felt compelled to investigate the commotion. Though still weak, he opened the tent's flap and saw several women forming a circle around two young Indians rolling in the dust. A knife flashed in the setting sun. Several Indian women pulled at the large boy with the knife, who now was on top of the other young man, the half-breed boy who had helped nurse David back to health. The knife-wielder swung his weapon menacingly at the women, driving them back in fear. He turned to the half-breed and drew his dagger back to strike it into the smaller boy's body.

David took several long strides forward and smashed his fist against the big boy's head. The boy and the knife flew in opposite directions. The boy landed on his hands and knees and shook his head for a clearer view of his assailant. David stood over him glaring in anger. In a flash, the boy lunged for the knife and charged at David. The women set up a background of frightened murmurings and moved away. The boy was shorter than David, but he was much heavier. David instinctively knew not to grapple with him in hand-to-hand combat, as he recognized that his strength was no match for the raw power that now rushed at him. Swiftly, and without time to think further, David stepped aside and kicked the boy in the groin. The boy hesitated for a split second and then slumped to his knees in intense pain, the knife still clutched in his hand.

His face was contorted with pain, but he began to rise slowly as

David was suddenly on him in a violent assault. Hitting and kicking, he forced the boy to the ground as he wrenched the knife away. Holding the flat blade in his hand, he hammered the boy's face with the handle of the large knife. Again and again he hit him, while grunting and breathing in short, quick gasps. Just as suddenly as he had launched the attack, his body froze with the knife raised for yet another smash. Sane consciousness returned, and the entire scene appeared completely unreal to David. He hardly knew what had happened. He rose quickly while the boy fought for breath. Blood flowed from the Indian's nose, cheeks, and eyes. David staggered to his tent and collapsed on his bedroll.

That night, the mother of the half-breed told her trapper husband of the incident and asked, "I thought you said that white man was a God man."

"That's what the hunters said," he replied.

"I never saw a God man fight like that."

"Yeah, but he saved our boy, didn't he?"

"Uh-huh, but you'd better watch out for him while he's here. He's mean. I wouldn't trust him if gets angry."

She paused a moment and then added, "I liked him better when he was sick."

Both David and the Indian boy recovered from the brief and violent encounter to discover that the trapper's family had given the attacker their everlasting enmity, and David their eternal thanks. They assured David that on any future visit to the West he could find a welcome in their wilderness home.

David made his weary way home in August. Ann made a cot for him in the cellar where it was cool, and she fed him six times a day. A slight wheezing in his chest persisted, but otherwise he slowly gained weight and strength. Incredibly, he began to plan his return to the Indians and the challenge of the native westerners. David had an inner calm assurance; he had espoused early a cause in which he fully believed until his dying day. That cause was the cause of Christ, and he never doubted for a moment that he had chosen the proper, the only, way of life. He firmly believed he had chosen rightly, believed wisely, and would achieve success in his endeavors for Christ and the right. There are not many to whom such inner happiness is given.

By October, David was in Philadelphia receiving a letter of recommendation from the Baptist Association to return to the

Indians. He did not, however, receive official or financial support for his mission. His bitterness over having to return alone, without pledges of some follow-up work on the part of his denomination, was intense. Though most of his ministerial contemporaries agreed that the work was vital and immediate, they also pointed out that neither funds nor qualified missionaries existed at the moment. David pleaded for others to follow his example of missionary endeavor, but no others were willing to sacrifice family, money, and the pleasures of a more comfortable, civilized life just then. David returned to the Ohio country in the chill of early autumn.

A book of Indian words was made by the self-appointed missionary. He preached as often as possible, and he cared for the sick. His presence, his attitude, and his helpfulness in ministering to the Indians were appreciated everywhere he went. His message of Christ, however, was largely ignored. He kept a full diary of his accounts which was of use to later missionaries, but he slowly came to realize that his efforts at a permanent ministry were largely in vain. In early April, a messenger brought news that his son Joseph, almost five, was dead. His grief knew no bounds as he hiked alone in the woods for three days. Anguished cries for strength and courage went up to God. He was home by the end of the month to comfort and help his family, and he wrote a book of his travels and work in the western forests. Deep in his heart, he knew his labors were not in vain. Surely someone, someday, would take up that work, he thought.

While he had been away, political storm clouds continued to form over the American colonies. Resistance to the British imposition of the Stamp Act had been followed by colonial outbursts against the Townshend Revenue Acts. The Boston Massacre in 1770, the Tea Party in 1773, and the rise of American Committees of Correspondence and nonimportation agreements against British goods were answered by the English passage of the Coercive Acts of 1774. By these, the Boston port was closed, town meetings were suppressed, British soldiers were quartered in colonial buildings, and other laws odious to the colonials were issued from London. In September, 1774, the First Continental Congress was called by disgruntled Americans. Insurrection and revolt were in the air.

The sermon at Crosswicks on October 19, 1774, upset the delicate balance of British sympathizers and colonial protestors in the church membership. David's sermon concerned a subject's obligation of loyalty to his sovereign. He mounted the high pulpit and spoke in measured words. With his jaw firmly set and his eyes flashing, he chose his text from Romans, chapter 13, concerning obedience to political rulers.

"The very design of the higher political powers is to secure the property and promote the happiness of the whole community. By this we understand that 'higher powers' is the just, the good, the wholesome, and constitutional law of a land. No blanket acquiescence to any and all rulers was ever intended in the Bible. When wicked, oppressive rulers are unjust, some men have seen it as their duty to resist them.

"The British are not securing our property or promoting happiness among us. To the contrary, because of their actions we are a divided and frightened people. Our rights as Englishmen are violated when we are denied constitutional guarantees, and taxed without representation. . . ."

A stir of disapproval swept much of the audience. Children sitting in the balcony sat still and frightened as the tension in the air grew thick and heavy. David was making his official public stand with those who were protesting against the crown. Those who were, and would remain, loyal to the British were angered and humiliated that their pastor would use the sanctity of the pulpit to espouse his political views.

"No!" "Sedition!" "Scandalous!" The words came from indignant lips throughout the congregation. The service ended without prayer or song. David simply finished speaking, climbed down the pulpit stairs, and stalked defiantly outside. He stood near the gravestones of three of his children as several men approached him with quick steps. David spread his feet, squared his shoulders, and prepared to meet whatever attack came.

"For shame, Reverend Jones! To preach seditious slander against your king when you are a minister of the Bible! For shame!"

"How dare you, Jones!" "You have disgraced us, sir!" The voices were from angered men now gathering around David.

"I demand your resignation, sir!" Josiah Pitman's voice pierced through all the frenetic talk and movement. The women and children stood still after they exited from the church. Ann walked quickly through the crowd of men and stood by her husband.

David thrust out his chin toward Mr. Pitman and said, "Demand my resignation, do you? Well, Deacon Pitman, I demand yours!"

John Chafey moved a step toward David, thought better of it, stepped back, and spoke with hostile words: "You are a hired servant, Reverend Jones, and you have no right to demand anyone's resignation. You are on trial here. You have usurped your position today, and I'll see to it that you will not have another chance to preach disrespect and disobedience in this house of God."

David's countenance grew livid with rage. He shouted in Mr. Chafey's face as he stepped toward him: "I am most certainly not a hired servant of yours, sir. I am God's servant. God, and God alone, tells me what to preach and when to preach it, and no English sympathizing laymen will tell me what to say. And I'll preach here as long as God and the majority of the people leave me here. You and your British friends try to remove me from this church, and you'll have more than a handful of trouble from those who are for me."

Several voices of assent spoke up. Peter Stelle, a close friend, joined Ann by David's side and diverted him toward the parsonage. It was an ugly scene. Pitman and Chafey quickly realized that their majority was not sufficiently clear to create any further serious confrontation that day. Angry men with set jaws gathered their families and headed home in wagons and buggies.

The following months grew increasingly burdensome to the Jones family. British sympathizers in the area were numerous and strong. Many refused to speak to Ann as she shopped in Bordentown; church attendance dropped to half its former number; and some children were forbidden to play with Eleanor, Morgan, and Mary. Once, a threatening note was nailed to the oak in front of the parsonage by an unknown night rider. It was a long and difficult winter. On April 22, 1775, a rider announced the bloodshed between British troops and Massachusetts farmers. Two days later, David announced his resignation at Crosswicks Baptist Church.

The Jones family had anticipated its removal from the hotbed of British loyalists. A Welsh church northwest of Philadelphia was pastorless, and David had visited with the deacons relevant to his fulfilling that role. He had inherited one hundred British pounds sterling at the death of his father, and that was sufficient for the purchase of a small farm in the Great Valley of Pennsylvania near those Welsh friends. If the pastorate of the Baptist Church in the Great Valley worked out, so much the better, but it was obvious that their work in New Jersey was finished. There was one additional matter he must take care of before he left Crosswicks, however.

"David, I think you should leave well enough alone. Let's leave with whatever little peace there is left here. Why confront the Tories who say you are leaving because you are afraid of them? That's silly," Ann advised.

"I'm sick of whisperings and malicious gossip about my courage, and I am most certainly not afraid of those loud-mouthed British," he replied.

"I know you're not, love, but if you confront them at their own homes, there may be violence. You'll be on their property, and then remember, there has been bloodshed in Massachusetts. . . ."

"No, Ann. I'll not leave here like a dog with his tail between his legs. If they think I'll run and hide from them, they're badly mistaken. Let's let them tell me to my face what they've been whispering to old ladies, Annie. Then we'll see who's afraid."

"David, please, let's just go."

"No, Ann, not before I take myself a little ride."

Potential violence that would soon engulf the New Jersey countryside in full-scale war was in the air as Tories and patriots armed themselves and waited for personal direction. Such was the mood as David rode up to the Pitman farm. Josiah Pitman saw David coming and walked out to meet him. Jeremy, the eldest Pitman son, stood at the door with a musket, his face glowering in anger at the intruder.

"Get off my property, Reverend Jones!" Josiah's voice was calculated and firm, his eyes narrowed.

"I'll get off your property just as soon as you say to my face what you've been saying about me to your British friends."

There was a pause as Pitman searched for words, "Get off my property!"

"Well, well. So you don't deny it, do you, Deacon Pitman? Now how big a coward am I, sir? If you'd like to prove my cowardice, well, here I am."

"I'm not going to tell you again to get off my property. Now git!"

Jeremy put both hands on the loaded musket and stepped toward the two men. David leaned over in his saddle so that his face was nearer Pitman.

"I'll get just as soon as you and your other British sympathizers see that I'm leaving without fear. You and your bunch have the majority here in the Jerseys, but you'll be overcome shortly and this church will have allegiance only to colonials one day. Our cause is just, and we will be back, sir. We'll be back. And by the way, don't bother telling your friends I came. I'll do it myself right now."

David pulled the reins of his horse sharply to the left, making Pitman jump to avoid being trampled. He rode away at a gallop heading for the Chafeys, the Tapscotts, and other British loyalists in an angry, almost threatening good-bye. David rode up to each man in defiance, offered to prove his courage, and rode away with an angry satisfaction.

When he arrived home at the end of the day, he told Ann, "I'm ready to go now."

"It's a wonder you didn't get yourself killed, you crazy man," she said. There was a half smile on her face as she embraced him hard.

4

A Fighting Chaplain

The Jones family did not settle quickly or comfortably at the Baptist Church in the Great Valley. The people wanted him as their pastor, to be sure, and David did indicate that he would remain with them until he found a more permanent home and pastorate. Neither pastor nor people, however, could afford anticipation of a bright future when armed bands of men were shedding each other's blood all around them. Boston's garrison of British soldiers was under siege following a bloody battle on the heights overlooking Charleston. Colonial soldiers were attacking Canada, and a Virginian loyal to the crown, John Connally, was organizing other loyalists in military units in the back country of Virginia and Pennsylvania. Wild rumors arrived daily telling of Connally's approach to Philadelphia. Thankfully for the Joneses, Chester County, Pennsylvania, had a majority of colonials opposing the British, unlike that hotbed of Tories in the Jerseys.

When the news of Lexington and Concord reached Chester County, the County Committee of Safety voted unanimously that it was "the indispensable duty of all the freemen of the country immediately to form and enter into associations for the purpose of learning the military art." Within a week, almost every village green and common was the site of drilling soldiers. Some men, such as Anthony Wayne, drilled each day they could spare from other public duties, such as serving in the Pennsylvania Assembly. Patriotic ministers were expected to be present, to preach to the men, and to encourage them, but without bearing arms themselves. That was the sole realm of the laymen at the time, according to many. David disagreed with that philosophy; he was frustrated beyond words, a caged lion, pacing the small parlor of his new home.

"I didn't see a man among them who had ever drilled before.

When I marched with the Delaware militia, most of those pink cheeked, fuzzy-faced kids hadn't been born." His voice was a trifle too strong for his one-person audience, Ann, who remained discreetly silent.

"Just who said a minister couldn't fight?" he asked, continuing to pace, his face scowling in anger. Ann's squeaking rocker irritated David. She fanned herself to find some relief from the summer heat and fought down the temptation to speak.

"Just because I can preach and they can't doesn't mean they can do something I can't. Why should I be penalized for having more than one talent?" He hit the doorcasing lightly in frustration as he watched a wagon loaded with five young men headed south to the Lancaster road.

"Well, Ann. What can I do?" He turned to her as if she, alone, were responsible.

"You could use that one talent now and bide your time for the future," she said as she met his gaze.

"I want to fight now."

"There's no enemy to fight here at the moment, David, but there are quite a few friends who could use the confidence of the Bible about the fight that's coming."

He tried to hide the smile that spread slowly across his face, but it came anyway. Ann smiled in return.

"I hate to admit it, but I wish I'd thought to say that," he said, laughing. He gathered up some sheets of paper, a quill, and some ink, and walked outside to the first row of his small apple orchard. Sitting on the shady ground, he propped his back against the trunk of the nearest tree and began to jot down his thoughts about the biblical justifications for war. Ann poured a cool drink of water for him.

The Continental Congress proposed a day of prayer and fasting for July 20, 1775, as a means of invoking the favor of God on their cause. Ministers were asked to preach to troops and to other citizens, and the enthusiastic new pastor at Great Valley was chosen to speak at Tredyffryn in Chester County. Colonel Dewees marched most of his regiment to the log meetinghouse where eventually more than three hundred men stood in ranks, their only uniform clothing a white linen shirt. Many had neither musket nor pistol, while a few had swords; some had no weapon. Spectators filled the space between the soldiers and the small meetinghouse porch where

David and several others were seated. Others stood in wagons or sat on the grass behind the troops. It was unusually hot with the sun beating unmercifully on the soldiers and spectators. The clouds that often built up on warm Pennsylvania days had provided neither shade nor showers. The preliminaries were lengthy, but David stood at last in front of the small makeshift podium and began his sermon.

"When a people become voluntary slaves to sin; when it is esteemed a reproach to reverence and serve God; when profaneness and dissolute morals become fashionable; when pride and luxury predominate, we cannot expect such a nation to be long happy." His clear, baritone voice projected well over the large audience. Intensity of feeling was apparent in his words. His text was from Nehemiah 4:14, ". . . Be not ye afraid of them: remember the Lord, which is great and terrible, and fight for your brethren, your sons, and your daughters, your wives, and your houses."

The sermon was not long by standards of the day, perhaps in consideration of the mid-day heat, but David covered three subjects thoroughly. He announced that "an endeavor shall be made to prove, that in some cases, when a people are oppressed, insulted and abased, and can have no other redress, it then becomes our duty as men, with our eyes to God, to fight for our liberties and properties; or in other words, that a defensive war is sinless before God." Later, the published sermon took its name from that phrase and became "Defensive War in a Just Cause Sinless." As the sermon progressed, the attention and admiration of the crowd increased. He cited biblical and historical examples of defensive war, condemned the British for attempting to enslave the colonies, and reminded the crowd that God's power would sustain their cause if they were free from the evils of the enemy.

"We are called to fight for our brethren, our sons and our daughters, our wives and our houses; and if God forsake us, our slavery is sure. Many trust too much on the arm of flesh; but let us place all our confidence in God. . . . Nehemiah prays, but omits not the use of means, he sets a watch night and day to guard against the enemy, and every man is equipped for battle.

"If ever there was one time that called for more religion than another, this is the very time. And yet, alas! alas! how few are seeking God! How few are seeking their salvation, when death is even at the door, and all at stake! Let me therefore entreat you seriously to lay to heart the present state, and 'remember the Lord, which is great and terrible.' Amen."

Applause followed a brief silence as David was seated, but the sound swelled as those sitting rose to their feet clapping. Scattered cries, "Hurrah for the Reverend," were heard on all sides as many in the crowd surrounded David uttering congratulations for a job well done. Ann worked her way to David and stood by his side beaming with pride.

"Reverend Jones, that sermon must be published." Dozens of voices spoke up in assent.

"We should distribute that message to every Continental militia unit in the army. That sermon expresses the sentiment of every patriot in the country."

"Promise us, Reverend Jones, that you'll allow it to be published."

"You are needed as a chaplain, Reverend."

The voices were eager and sincere. David smiled and nodded his permission to allow his words to be printed if those around him desired. Within a few weeks, David's sermon was printed and distributed up and down the Atlantic seaboard, drawing praise from those in rebellion and vitriolic criticism from the Tories and the British.

The published sermon was a seven-page argument for the right to fight against Great Britain. In addition to the scriptural arguments, mainly drawn from the Old Testament, David dealt with several objections to taking up arms againt the British. He denied, for example, that the scriptural admonition to "obey the higher powers" meant a blanket obedience to any and all rulers. David felt that the only rulers worthy of obedience were just rulers.

He also explained that martial engagements do suit a meek and loving disciple of Jesus in that all people on earth are not Christians and therefore cannot be expected to be treated as Christians. Though some of the patriots might have questioned his logic, none of them resented his pointing out some of the dangers that faced the patriot cause.

"Remember our Congress is in imminent danger. It is composed of men of equal characters and fortunes of most, if not superior to any in North America—These worthy gentlemen have ventured all in the cause of liberty for our sakes;—if we were to forsake them, they must be abandoned to the rage of a relentless ministry. Some of them are already proscribed, and no doubt this would be the fate of the rest: How could we bear to see these worthy patriots hanged as criminals of the deepest dye? Their families plundered of all they possess, and abandoned to distress and poverty?"

David also warned of what might befall the readers' sons and daughters as he added: "Your sons and your daughters must be strangers to the comforts of liberty;—they will be considered like beasts of burden, only made for their masters' use. If the groans and cries of posterity in oppression can be any argument, come now, my noble countrymen, fight for your sons and your daughters. But if this will not alarm you, consider what will be the case of your wives, if a noble resistance is not made: all your estates confiscated, and distributed to the favourites of arbitrary power, your wives must be left to distress and poverty. This might be the better endured, only the most worthy and flower of all the land shall be hanged, and widowhood and poverty both come in one day."

He closed with a defense of the patriot cause and an appeal to be worthy of God's blessings of victory by living righteous lives: "Our present dispute is just, our cause is good.—We have been as loyal subjects as any on earth;—at all times, when occasion called, we have contributed towards the expense of war with liberal hands, beyond our power, even in their estimation. When we have been called to venture our lives in defense of our king and country, have we refused? No, verily; we have been willing to spill our precious blood. We have been charged with designs of independency: This possibly may be the event, but surely against our wills; the decent addresses to his Majesty, as well as all other prudential measures, are arguments in our favour. But all our measures are disregarded, the terms offered us are but a few degrees milder than what the Ammonites offered to Jabesh-Gilead. . . . And if we are successful in our present struggle for liberty, we cannot expect to enjoy any lasting happiness without a reformation, and a life worthy of the glorious gospel."

The fact that some felt the sting of his words stimulated David. He had always enjoyed a good fight, and now he was entering an armed arena which was to satisfy his desire for conflict to the fullest.

The period of uncertainty and indecision concerning the war between two opposing forces came to a swift end. The Second Continental Congress, meeting in Philadelphia in the autumn of 1775, laid plans for an offensive, as well as a defensive war. English reinforcements for the besieged Boston troops were also on the way as military strategy and tactics were being swept along by the moving tides of minor skirmishes turned to full-scale warfare. As early as May 10, 1775, the British fort on Lake Champlain, Fort Ticonderoga, fell to Benedict Arnold, Ethan Allen, and his "Green Mountain Boys." Cannon from the fort were hauled by patriot General Knox over rugged, snow-covered New York mountains later in the winter for the siege of the British army now bottled up in Boston. In February, 1776, the siege began in earnest just as news from the south told of Virginia's Lord Dunmore's defeat by patriots at Norfolk. Two small Continental armies attacked Canada in the fall of 1775 to complete the American strategy.

The British soon evacuated Boston and moved on to New York, however, where General Washington hurried to form a makeshift defense. Men of all the colonies had decisions to make concerning the correctness of rebellion or the necessity to remain loyal to their king. Neutrality was difficult, but for David's allegiance there never had been a moment's hesitation. He had sympathized with the early protests against the British, and he lost no time in declaring himself for the rebels in what he termed "our civil war." He was willing to preach his sentiments when there was no warfare, but now that battles were being fought all around him, he determined to be a part of the conflict. The chaplaincy was an obvious way to combine his calling and his desire to be a part of the fighting. He offered his services to the Pennsylvania Assembly and was immediately appointed as a chaplain to the Fourth Pennsylvania Battalion on April 27, 1776. His unit was ordered to Fort Ticonderoga to support the harassed American army retreating from a disastrous defeat at Quebec.

David said good-bye to each of the four children in the house. "Annie, will you walk to the top of the hill with me? Eleanor and Mary can watch the boys."

Ann took David's free hand as he led the horse away from the house. Ann's throat was choked with emotion. She couldn't speak.

"I know you're thinking of the last time I was gone, Annie, when little Joseph left us."

Ann broke into sobs, and David put his arm around her as they walked. The memory of those lonely hours welled up in her mind. Her dead baby, her husband out in the wilderness. . . . *Oh, please God, don't let it happen again,* she thought.

"We're all involved in this war, Annie. This time you and the children may be in danger if I don't go help stop the British."

They stopped at the crest of the hill and looked back toward the house, mostly hidden in the trees. He released her hand and checked his horse and equipment. He patted his long musket tied to the side of the saddle and tightened the cinch. It was time to mount, but he couldn't think of a proper good-bye to his grieving wife. He put his arms around her. She cried softly for several minutes.

"'R wyn dy garu, Anniefach."

"I love you, too, David. Oh, how I love you."

They looked at each other as Ann wiped her tears on her handkerchief. She regained her composure and in her inimitable way tried to say something to lighten the pain of leaving with a word of humor.

"Do you think you can keep up with those fuzzy-cheeked boys? You're almost forty years old, you know!"

David smiled, relieved that the emotional tension had passed.

"Yeah, I'll keep up with them. They might even have to strain a bit to keep up with me."

They both laughed. There was a pause and then David pressed his

wife close to him, mounted his horse, and was off to a long and bitter war. Though never far away in miles, he would be home for only brief visits during the next seven years.

He actually enjoyed the trip up the Hudson River to Lake George. The delays in the New York City area had been frustrating, but now he was viewing places he had only heard about before. The mountains in upper New York were rugged and beautiful to his eye, as were the streams and lakes. Bright flowers and ferns were in full bloom in July, 1776, as the Fourth Pennsylvania Battalion reached "Ti," as the soldiers called Fort Ticonderoga. Tension mounted as word was received that British troops were in hot pursuit of the retreating colonials. A stand would be made at "Ti," and these Pennsylvanians were the support troops desperately needed to stop the onrushing redcoats.

All hands were thrown immediately into repairing and reinforcing the fortifications. Old gun emplacements were filled with stones and mortar as the few cannons were trained on the waterways leading to the fort from the north, east, and south. Fort "Ti" was situated at the southern end of Lake Champlain and the northern boundary of Lake George, so that an attack by water was highly probable. The western approach to the defense was manned by infantry. David preached on Sundays and ministered at frequent burials recurring with alarming frequency as wounded and sick succumbed. Overcrowding, lack of medicines, shortages of food, and lack of adequate shelter added great fuel to the plague of smallpox now ravaging the camp. David was called on frequently to assist the doctors and surgeons in their almost hopeless task to fight off the most formidable enemy of all in this war—death. The long delays passed into sleepless weeks as the British neared Fort Ticonderoga.

"David Jones, Chaplain, Fourth Pennsylvania, reporting as ordered, sir." David stood at attention in front of the table set up outside in the warm sunshine of early autumn. Several officers stood to the side discussing the contents of a large roll of paper, obviously a map.

"Thank you for coming, Chaplain. I have need of your services for purposes other than you intended when you came to reinforce us, and I felt that I should speak to you personally about the matter. Won't you be seated, please?"

Colonel Anthony Wayne motioned to a chair in front of the table. The two men made a striking contrast. Though from the same section of Pennsylvania, their physical characteristics were entirely different. David's tall, thin frame accentuated Colonel Wayne's shorter, stockier build. Whereas David combed his long, straight black hair toward the back of his head and tied it tightly with a small ribbon, Colonel Wayne's hair tended to curl out in all directions, not in an unkempt fashion, but neither was it quite neat and tidy.

"Our medical situation, as you have undoubtedly noticed, Jones, is becoming perilous. I understand you are a trained doctor?"

"Well, yes, sir, I did train to be a doctor, but in the Jerseys they will not recognize doctors who have not taken examinations, and I never took them."

"But you did receive medical training?"

"Yes, sir, I did."

"My medical staff tells me you are as capable as they in both medication and surgery."

"Thank you, sir."

"Reverend Jones, I will not order you to change your duties from those of a chaplain to those of a doctor, but I do need your help. Will you retain your commission as a chaplain and serve with my medical unit, too? Please be honest with me as to your thoughts on this affair."

"Sir, I will help wherever I can be of help. If you feel that I am needed with the medical unit, then I'll be happy to serve with them."

"All right, Chaplain, that's good. Let's do it this way. Until you hear otherwise from me, work with Dr. Battina as much as you can. Preach whenever you can, and try to work out your schedule with him. If you have any problems, deal directly with me. We won't change your commission, but you will assume both duties as of now. Is that agreeable with you?"

"Quite agreeable, sir."

"Very well. I'll have the adjutant assign your duties with Battalion Medical as well as with my staff as chaplain. And thank you, Chaplain."

David was later cleaning surgical equipment when the news arrived that the English general, Carleton, had left Crown Point for an attack on "Ti." Carleton had defeated the small American fleet on Lake Champlain on October 11, and now he had no major hindrance between his forces and the waiting Americans. General St. Clair's brigade was assembled for a message from their chaplain prior to assuming their places in the lines of defense. Chaplain Jones was not unprepared for the message, for he had added to his "war message" often in anticipation of just such an exigency. The men were in full battle dress as David's voice rose over the parade ground.

"My countrymen, Fellow-soldiers, and Friends. I am sorry that during this campaign I have been favored with so few opportunities of addressing you on subjects of the greatest importance both with respect to this life and that which is to come. But what is past cannot be recalled. Therefore at present let it suffice to bring to your remembrance some necessary truths.

"It is our common faith that all events on earth are under the notice of that God in whom we live, move, and have our being. Thus, we must believe that God has assigned us our post here at Ticonderoga. Here we can give our enemies a fatal blow, and in great measure prove the means of the salvation of North America."

He appealed to their natural hatred of the hired German mercenaries, called Hessians, as he pointed to the fact that men were approaching who "would cut your throats for the small reward of sixpence." Waxing ever more eloquent, he reminded them of their loved ones at home and the threats they faced, as was his custom during each message.

"See, Oh! see the dear wives of your bosoms forced from their peaceful habitations, and perhaps used with such indecency that modesty would forbid description! Behold the fair virgins of your land, whose benevolent souls are now filled with a thousand good wishes and hopes of seeing their admirers return home crowned with victory. See your children exposed as vagabonds to all calamities of this life! Then, Oh! then adieu to all felicity this side of the grave!

"Now all these calamities may be prevented if our God be for us— and who can doubt of this who observes the point in which the wind now blows—if you will only acquit yourselves like men. Go forth against your enemies, resolving either to return with victory or to die gloriously. Everyone that may fall in this dispute will be justly esteemed a martyr of liberty, and his name will be had in precious memory while the love of freedom remains in the breasts of men.

"As our present case is singular, I hope, therefore, that the candid will excuse me, if I now conclude with an uncommon address. It is in substance principally extracted from the writings of the servants of God in the Old Testament; though at the same time, it is freely acknowledged that I am not possessed of any similar power either of blessing or cursing.

"Blessed be the man who is possessed of true love of liberty; and let all the people say . . ." David hesitated, and the men all shouted in response—"Amen!"

"Blessed be the man who is a friend to the United States of America; and let all the people say . . ." Again, there was a resounding "Amen!"

"Blessed be the man who is resolved never to submit to Great Britain; and let all the people say . . ." "Amen!"

"Let him be an outcast, a terror to himself and to all around him." "Amen!"

The crack of rifle fire was heard in the meadow beyond the walls.

"Let him who deserts the noble cause in retreat be abhorred by all the United States of America." "Amen!"

"Let him be cursed in all his connections, till his wretched head with dishonor is laid low in the dust; and let all the soldiers shout . . ." "Amen!"

David's voice was high and piercing through the growing anxiety of the enemy's approach.

"And may the God of all grace, in whom we live, enable us, in defense of our country, to acquit ourselves like men, to his honor and praise forever. Amen and Amen."

"Amen!" "Amen!" "Amen!" shouted the soldiers.

The fight that day was small in comparison to later battles, but some men who stood in the ranks responding to the chaplain with loud, hearty "amens" died that afternoon. David's voice, encouraging them to honor God, family, and country, was one of the last voices to entreat them. General Carleton surveyed the fort, still intact after the brief attack, counted his losses, and withdrew his troops to Canada and winter quarters.

David's sermon at Ticonderoga was printed later in the winter as illustrative of a good chaplain's admonition to troops ready to enter combat, but David was too busy with the sick and wounded to take much notice of his second publication. A message from home told of Ann's expecting another child while David was acting as a messenger for General Wayne. David was used in the capacity of a messenger because little information was passing from "Ti" to New York and Philadelphia due to enemy activity between the two American forces and the supply lines to the south. Several couriers were killed and captured, frustrating the officers at Fort Ticondero-ga. David finally volunteered to act as a messenger and guarantee that dispatches reached their destination. General Wayne agreed that his chaplain just might be successful, and hence gave the following message to David to be delivered to Benjamin Franklin:

"Dear Sir: We are so far removed from the seat of Government or the free and independent states of America—and such an insurmountable barrier, Albany, between us that not one letter, or the least intelligence of anything that's doing with you can reach us. Through the medium of my chaplain (David Jones), I hope this will reach you as he has promised to blow out any man's brains who will attempt to take it from him. . . ."

The bold and adventurous chaplain evidently delivered the message without incident, for when he returned, he plunged into his duties as a doctor without further mention of the journey. The condition of the men in the midst of a hard Adirondack winter was abominable. The entire camp had only flour and pork to eat, and there was not enough wood in the nearby meadows to cook even that. Half of the men, only, had shoes, and few blankets existed to cover their thin shirts and trousers. Medicines were soon exhausted, while the few surgeons were bone weary, with double duty the order of every day. Then the dreaded medical enemy hit with full fury—smallpox. The groans and moans of sick and dying men tortured by the burning and itching of that loathsome disease could be heard everywhere. They died like flies, their corpses wrapped in their filthy clothes and pushed into snowbanks to await a decent burial that the spring thaws would provide.

The sights and sounds of that pest-ridden fort were unbearable to many of the men. Some healthy officers, unable any longer to stand the sufferings of others, gathered in small groups and deliberately drank themselves into insensibility. The worst of the sick were loaded into small boats, with the "best" of them pulling the oars. David helped load the boats with whatever food could be secured and pointed them southward toward whatever help they could find. When most of the sick and badly wounded had been moved out, David received orders to accompany the last group to Washington's winter quarters at Morristown, New Jersey. He arrived there in a March snowstorm, fatigued, hungry, pale, extremely thin, coughing and wheezing, but still on his feet. His first full campaign had been a bitter test of will, courage, and physical endurance. He doubted that he could endure another such expedition.

It was a recuperating army that David joined in the mountains near Morristown. Washington had been driven from New York in 1776, pushed across New Jersey with a terrible loss of men killed and captured, and the loss of much of his equipment at Forts Lee and Washington on the Hudson River. The Continental Army did win a smashing victory at Trenton on Christmas night as they recrossed the Delaware River and routed General Raal's Hessian mercenaries. Moving eastward again, Washington defeated the British at Princeton, but was forced into winter quarters with a weary, though unbowed, army. By the time David arrived, enlistments were increasing, and the army was growing stronger. Since matters were improving at Morristown, David asked for and received leave for a visit home when he was physically able to travel. He had been gone for a year, needing now the nursing of body, mind, and soul that only a loving family and friends can give. Besides, he was anxious to greet his new son, named Horatio Gates Jones in honor of David's new friend, General Horatio Gates of the northern army.

The Baptist Church in the Great Valley had secured a supply preacher, Reverend Thomas Jones, to minister to them in David's absence, and on his leave, David was invited to preach several Sundays in his church. Though David had agreed to serve the church for only one year when he arrived in April, 1775, the church considered him as their pastor on temporary leave to the army. David's strength grew as he awaited developments from Morristown. He helped some with spring ploughing, purchased and mixed medicines in preparation for the summer's campaign, and reported his unit's activities at Ticonderoga to many interested groups.

In April, 1777, he received word from his unit that there was a possibility for the British to attack Philadelphia. If so, the message stated, he should remain at home until the army marched toward him. He could unite with them near his home at the appropriate time.

The thought that the war might engulf his own family near Philadelphia paralyzed David with fear. He anxiously awaited the location of the British army that sailed from New York in June. Would they move north toward New England? Perhaps they would attack in the south? A hard-riding courier brought the news that the

British fleet had deposited the main body of the British army at the head of the Chesapeake Bay in Maryland, and they were marching toward Delaware and Philadelphia. The next day a message arrived for David: "Report to General Wayne immediately."

Following the assignment as a scout in Delaware and the fight at Cooch's Bridge near the Welsh Tract Baptist Church, David reported back to his own unit moving up Brandywine Creek during the second week of September, 1777. There was some confusion among the American army as units hurried to join the main body of troops, and Washington struggled to keep his army between the British and Philadelphia, the avowed object of the English strategy. The Americans moved northward along the Brandywine and probed the enemy with patrols, while General Howe's redcoats searched for a suitable place to cross the creek and engage Washington. It became obvious to all that a major battle would occur soon, its outcome determining the fate of Philadelphia, the new capitol.

Brandywine Creek empties into the Delaware River at Wilmington, Delaware, after flowing from its source in the Pennsylvania mountains some twenty-two miles to the northwest. Approximately ten miles above Wilmington the stream alternately narrows into a rushing current and widens into long, flat, placid flows. Four fords, or easily crossed shallows, were formed in those wide areas. Within the space of two-and-one-half miles, four fords were known to be accessible to Howe's approaching army; Jones's Ford was on the upstream, or northwestern, end of the four; Brinton's, Chadd's, and Pyle's fords ended that downstream section of passable areas. General Howe's main body of troops were marching down the road leading directly to Chadd's Ford. On the American left, Pyle's Ford lay beside a narrow, roaring gully with the banks extremely precipitous and well-wooded.

Since that ford was easily defended, Washington placed a militia unit there under the command of General John Armstrong. These volunteers who had not experienced combat would be out of the way of the more serious fighting, while General Sullivan's regulars were placed upstream to cover Jones's and Brinton's fords. General Greene's units were on the heights above the creek in reserve, leaving General Anthony Wayne, with Proctor's Artillery, at Chadd's Ford. These troops would bear the brunt of the expected British attack, and well they should. All the troops of Wayne's command had experienced combat previously, but even more important reasons dictated their position. General Wayne had proven himself a capable organizer and a man known not so much for maneuvering as for fighting. In addition, these men were Pennsylvanians—many, like David, with their wives and children only a few miles away. That these veterans would fight to the last extremity was well known and appreciated by the commander. General Wayne placed his troops in line and rode up and down snapping orders to subordinates, assuring himself that all was in readiness for the British soldiers whose approach was heralded by a cloud of dust.

David had no medical duties to attend to at the moment; so as chaplain of the regimental staff, he remained close by General Wayne ready to assist with relaying messages or personal assistance to the general, should he be wounded. He watched across the creek as rank upon rank of red-coated British took up positions just out of effective artillery range. His anger grew to almost uncontrollable rage as he recognized the German tongue when orders were shouted. These were the Hessians—mercenaries, those who would slit your throat for sixpence. These were the barbarians who bayoneted poor helpless militia boys trying to surrender on Long Island. These were the brutalizers who would rather stab a boy than shoot a man. Rapists. Hired killers. He calmed his anger into a quiet hatred.

Brandywine Battle Site

From deep within his throat, he growled in his native Welsh, "Dihiryn. Moch. Moch brunt." ("Rascals. Pigs. Dirty Pigs.")

David reached for his pistol and started for the creek as the redcoats moved forward. American artillery belched smoke and flame from the high hills behind David as gaps appeared in the British lines. They stopped, re-formed, and moved toward the creek once more. The Pennsylvania Line aimed its muskets at the spot on the Hessian soldiers where their two white straps crossed just below their breast bones. The red ranks now stepped into the water.

"Fire!" General Wayne screamed beside David.

The Americans fired at their white-crossed targets. American soldiers were trained to fire at specific targets far more than their enemy, who fired not at targets, but in volleys directly in front of each rank. As a result of their attempts to cover a specific area in front of them, they often fired at gaps in the American lines, or they fired too high or too low. On Brandywine Creek, each American fired at the white cross directly in front of him. Sometimes several bullets found their mark in a single man. The fire of the musketry was devastating. The front rank of the Hessians slowed, stopped, and then appeared to fall into the creek as a unit. The waters turned red. The artillery was adjusted downward and joined the rifles and muskets in reaping death and destruction from the remains of the first British rank. The few stragglers backed away slowly and in good order as the Pennsylvania Line reloaded.

"General Wayne, the British have divided their command, and General Washington says to attack across the ford immediately." The rider was breathless and wild-eyed as he rode up to the staff.

"Where are the other British?"

"I don't know, sir, but the general said only General Knyphausen's Hessians are in front of you. Generals Sullivan and Armstrong will close on their flanks."

"Tell Colonel Shelton to move the Second across." Wayne turned to a dispatcher.

"Glory be to God, General. We just may end the Hessians once and for all!" David spoke exuberantly as a huge grin spread across his face. He rode down toward the water for a better view. The remainder of the staff continued exchanging messages. A few moments later, completely unknown to David, another rider rode up to General Wayne's group with an alarming message.

"General Wayne, the British have turned our right flank and

they're moving to your rear. General Washington orders an immediate withdrawal. Sullivan is routed on your right, sir."

"What?" The rider repeated his message. The small group now heard a growing fight to their right over the hills. The artillerymen on the heights were gesturing wildly toward Wayne, as the staff rode to higher ground for a better view. What they saw made General Wayne's emotions approach numbing fear. Not more than two hundred yards to the north, Sullivan's troops were retreating in confusion. Beyond them, thousands of British were charging the frail rear guards with bayonets. The left line of the redcoats had swept so far to the east that the Philadelphia Road was about to be cut off. The Americans would soon be surrounded. If escape were at all possible, they would have to fight their way to the rear.

"So that's where the British were? Knyphausen was the decoy and we fell right into the trap!" Wayne's grasp of the situation was immediate.

"Rider, stop Shelton's troops immediately or all will be lost. Turn the pieces east," he waved at the artillery captain who rode up. "Form lines on the hill, Major, and be ready to move out in good order." His voice had the faint trace of desperation.

Meanwhile, unaware that disaster lurked within a few hundred yards, David watched Colonel Shelton's regiment stride forward into the water as weak, sporadic firing from the British answered their charge. Because of the dust and smoke, David did not see several riders dash their mounts into the water with the command from General Wayne to retreat, and do it fast. What he did see was rank upon rank of seasoned troops falling back in the face of extremely light enemy resistance. He was incredulous.

"What are you doing?" he shouted. "Why are you running? Stand and fight; the enemy is ours!"

He spurred his horse into the stream, pleading with the men to form ranks to the front.

"Where are the officers? Fight, men!"

He was facing the retreating Americans as he shouted. Bullets whizzed all around him. Not knowing that the order of retreat had been given, he was completely confused. He turned in midstream and saw a perfectly formed rank of Hessians with muskets pointed straight ahead. Not more than twenty yards from them, he was in their direct line of fire. No other American was clear of the smoke and dust except David; they had all retreated.

"Feuer!" ("Fire!")

David lost his sense of proportion. The trees, the Hessians, his horse, the water—all became distorted. Strangely, the water appeared to be coming up to slap him in the face. When he gasped for air, he half filled his lungs with liquid. Where was he? He needed air. His horse was pinning him under the water; that was it, he thought. *I must be shot, but where? They couldn't have missed at that range.* The horse thrashed wildly in the stream. David stood up in knee-deep water toward the American side, his pistol still in his hand. A glance showed the horse's left front leg almost shot away. He saw the Hessians, with fixed bayonets, advance toward him. He raised his pistol, still struggling for air, took aim, and fired. The wet powder was useless, of course. He hesitated briefly, then threw the pistol at the nearest trooper and scurried toward the safety of the American side of the creek. As he ran, he felt for wounds that must surely be there, but there were none. Miraculously, he had escaped death at the Battle of Brandywine.

Somehow David made it back to the American lines which had re-formed and were holding off the enemy from both the north and the west. After dark, they were able to pull back toward Philadelphia, as General Greene's reserves had cleared out the British in the rear of the Philadelphia Line. Sick at heart over the crushing defeat, realizing that the enemy could easily be in his home tonight if they wished, David plodded along with the returning troops on foot. His body was weary, his horse and equipment were gone, but his hatred of his enemy sustained him as he sought to find the medical unit. He had seen many a torn and mangled body today, and he knew there would be a need for many doctors tonight.

The Fourth Pennsylvania medical detachment occupied a residence recently vacated by Tories fleeing before the retreating Continental Army. For three days and nights, David assisted in the surgical removal of wounded limbs while administering medications in a desperate fight against infection.

The surgical practices of the day were extremely crude, made necessary by lack of scientific knowledge, the necessary haste of battle, and poor equipment. The first process involved in treating a wounded man was the removal of a bullet. Since the point of entry into the body was obviously where the blood flowed, only two instruments were used to remove the large lead intruder. First, a long, narrow "U"-shaped scoop with a sharp point was thrust down into the wound, twisting and turning until the bullet was struck. Holding the scoop with one hand, a thin, razor-sharp knife was run down the concave scoop with the other hand, slicing upward and outward through huge amounts of flesh. When the knife reached the bullet, the surgeon lifted the lead out by pushing it up through the torn and bleeding slit. The wound was allowed to bleed, since the flow would, hopefully, wash away the infection. Compress bandages were then tied tightly to the area with hope that the bleeding would soon stop without the telltale signs of discoloration of flesh that would signal the next step in the surgical process.

There was only one "sure cure" for infection known at the time— amputation. Again, the doctors' equipment was most primitive in design and function. Sharp razors, knives, and saws made the amputation, with common thread and needles and large metal clamps used to close the wound as best they could. The entire process of infection fighting then began anew with the probability of death quite high. There was little anesthesia to deaden the pain and that was limited to alcohol and a few drugs when they were available. Lucky was the man who fainted at some point during the operation. Many, of course, never awakened from their unconscious state.

While in Philadelphia, David was used in each of the processes, but as time wore on, he became more involved in amputations. As with the other doctors, his patients' rate of recovery was poor. Soldier after suffering soldier lay in a raging fever as cold packs and various medicines were tried in an effort to abate the killing body heat. After all his known resources were exhausted, David often knelt beside a groaning, delirious man and prayed for God to intercede with a miracle. More deaths than miracles followed, however.

When the deaths did occur, David removed his stained surgical garments and donned his officer's uniform without epaulets, picked up his Bible, and conducted a brief funeral service beside an open grave. He was too weary with his back-breaking schedule to hear some of his officer friends quip that if wounded they would prefer to be doctored by someone other than David. "After all," their macabre joke went, "I'd prefer to risk my chances with someone who won't get a funeral fee if he operates on me unsuccessfully!" Chaplains did not, of course, receive funeral fees, and when David at last overheard the caustic teasing, he reacted in typical fashion; he gave the smiling jokester a tongue-lashing he would not forget. Yet when David walked the streets of Philadelphia alone that night, his eyes filled with tears as he experienced bitter resentment at any suggestion that he failed to do his best in every situation. He had not volunteered to be a doctor; he was asked to do so by his commander. David had suffered, and would continue to suffer, stings of hurt pride when anyone did not approve of him or of his work.

The morning following his long walk, Joseph, the family servant, arrived from the farm bringing a horse, fresh clothes, and a delicious chocolate cake. A note from Ann accompanied the welcome gifts from home.

"Dearest David, Please be assured that though the battles go badly for you and for all of us, we are all as well as can be expected here at home. The corn is shucked and stacked, the garden is still bringing in vegetables daily, and we have arranged to go stay with the Councilmans if the British get any nearer. We all love you very much, David. You will be pleased to know that Eleanor has been a godsend to all of us. She is a very mature fourteen-year-old. Mary and Morgan do their share, and David is still coughing, but he is no worse, I suppose. Little Horatio is being spoiled by all the others. We're all fine, David.

"Joseph has been a big help, and I want him to stay with you. That way you can send him home for anything you need. The message said you were not hurt—Oh, David, please, please take care of yourself. What happened to Dunny? Was he killed or did the British get him? We hear that the redcoats are gathering up all the horses they can lay their stealing hands on; so I guess they got him if he's still alive. We love you, David. God bless you and keep you in his power and safety. We will be here when you come home. Ann."

The Welsh of Delaware and Pennsylvania had seldom practiced the ownership of black slaves. The Jones family had never possessed slaves, but David and Ann did hire a black freedman, Joseph, when David left for his missionary journeys in the west. He was a great help to Ann and the children during David's protracted absences as he helped with the farming and chores around the house. Joseph was left without parents, due to a smallpox epidemic in Philadelphia, and was eager to live and work with a family in the fresh air of the country. He was a stout boy of sixteen when he came to them, and now at twenty-one he was an integral and important part of the family. David was extremely pleased to have him and the encouraging words from Ann. Yet the British were out there foraging, robbing, and harassing the farms of Chester County, and David feared for the safety of his family. He turned to the sick and injured as a remedy for his fears.

Orders arrived on September 13 for David to rejoin his unit as they marched out of Philadelphia to attempt battle with the British. On Lancaster Road, twenty-two miles west of the city, battle lines were drawn for another major conflagration as David prepared his medical kit. Not more than five miles from his home, the Pennsylvania Line was moving forward with sporadic firing as a torrential rainstorm descended. A heavy cloud cover had moved up and down the Atlantic coastline with the black, rain-laden clouds unloading their wet burden amidst cyclonic winds. For twenty-four hours the furious rainfall prohibited any fighting or movement by either side.

The ammunition wagons of both armies were soaked beyond hope of immediate use. Wading cold streams chest and neck deep, the American army pulled back to find a suitable crossing of the Schuylkill River. Their strategy was to keep themselves between the British and Philadelphia, but the weather and lack of equipment was making that task increasingly difficult. Washington would need to exert great caution in maneuvering his army to keep from being pinned with his back to the Delaware River with a superior force in front of him.

Anthony Wayne was detached from the main army at this point for an important and highly secretive mission. Taking fifteen hundred men and four fieldpieces with him, he was to fall in the rear of the British army and attempt to cut off their baggage train. Thus, delayed by lack of supplies, the enemy could not forbid the passage of the Americans across the Schuylkill. The element of surprise was to be their major asset, for if discovered, the huge British army could turn on them with a vengeance. David and one other doctor were assigned to accompany the small strike force. During the night of September 18 the unit marched quietly out of camp. Their equipment was strapped down tightly to still the normal rattling and clanging of moving soldiers. They marched all night with orders whispered up and down the long lines as they slowly moved to the rear of the British army. Just before dawn of the nineteenth, they encamped in a large clump of woods between the Paoli and Warren

Monument on Site of Paoli Massacre

taverns. Scouts reported the British four miles to the northeast preparing to move out to the Schuylkill.

The critical situation of his troops caused General Wayne to write a dispatch to Washington asking for General William Smallwood's promised reinforcements. The troops lay in the woods all during the overcast day. Observing the British readying to break camp the next morning, Wayne sent a rider galloping off to hurry Smallwood and then held a meeting with his officers. As soon as the main body of the British began their march, Wayne's troops would dash in among the rear guard and supply trains. Capturing and burning as much of the train as possible, they would beat a hasty retreat eastward away from Washington, hoping that General Howe would follow their fast-moving force. No evidence indicated that the British knew a deadly threat lay in the woods just beyond their rear guard.

It was impossible, however, to hide fifteen hundred men and equipment in an area abounding with British loyalists. Unknown to Wayne, a nearby farmer had been awakened by the passing American columns two nights earlier. He saddled his horse, followed the army at a discreet distance, and watched them camp in the woods near Paoli Tavern. By mid-morning he had ridden into the British camp, disclosing the location, approximate number, and major equipment of the Americans. General Howe quickly prepared a surprise of his own. Ordering General Grey to assemble three thousand men, Howe planned an assault on the hidden Americans at midnight. No artillery was to be taken; only unloaded muskets with bayonets were to be used, with a Hessian battalion taking the lead. The troops were to weave their way into the American lines and use only the sword and bayonet. The element of surprise now passed from the Americans to the British.

David stood outside the two small tents where several sick soldiers lay breathing heavily. The cold, damp air following exposure to rain and lack of food and clothing had caused a high fever and vomiting among some of the troops. It was almost dark, and David was tired and exasperated that these men would be useless tomorrow when they were needed in the attack. He knew he would have to remain behind with them, and his disappointment at missing the action exacerbated his weariness. David became aware of more than the usual activity around the camp.

"Why are the extra pickets being sent out, Joseph?" His servant was digging in a large sack for some item.

"I hear some British might attack us, Reverend Jones."

"I doubt that, Joseph. General Wayne just told some of us a while ago that there was no enemy movement." He paused. "Still, why don't you saddle up the horses and tighten the packs?"

David felt uneasy about something. The last of the soldiers were lying down around him in a perimeter near the tents as darkness crept slowly in. The pickets were out, and no enemy had been seen headed this way all day. Yet David felt a desire to go to the staff tent and see what he could find out. "Oh, well, I'm too tired for that," he thought to himself. "Besides, General Wayne will be prepared, I'm sure." He checked to see that all was in readiness as he lay down beside Joseph. Even then, a British force twice the size of Wayne's troops had completely encircled the sleeping Americans. They lay waiting for a midnight signal.

Those signals were whispered all around the hill as red-coated men grasped their muskets firmly and moved forward. The officers carried sabres as the British came bayoneting the outer line of pickets across the small meadow. Someone shouted. A shot was fired as the redcoats dashed in among the sleeping forms on the ground. David awoke with that wide-awake alertness that grips one's heart when danger is imminent. He leaped up to see several Hessians with peaked hats shove down the two tents where his sick men lay sleeping. Before he could mount his horse, the bayonets had pierced the bodies of those men, who only a moment before had lain beside him breathing unevenly. Screams and shouts now mixed with flashing swords, bayonets, gutteral curses, and grunts. Confused, half-clothed men ran in every direction attempting to escape the men in red with white belts who savagely thrust bayonets into those too slow to disentangle themselves from their blankets.

In the saddle, David saw a young soldier, backed up against a large tree, hold out his hands in a futile gesture to stave off the bayonet that was thrust toward his stomach. The Hessian shouted as he shoved the bayonet through his unarmed opponent. The boy's eyes opened in wide-eyed disbelief as an eerie cry came from his throat. The bayonet imbedded itself in the boy and the tree behind him. The Hessian cursed as he twisted the blade off the musket's sprocket, drew his sword, and dashed off for another victim. The boy struggled momentarily against his steel death trap, and then as blood gushed from his mouth and nostrils, he slumped across the blade, still pinned to the tree.

The neighing of David's and Joseph's horses as they were mounted attracted the attention of the British nearby who swung their bayonets toward the two mounted men. Without weapons, and with the enemy all around them, escape appeared impossible. The two men did the only thing that could have saved them for the moment. Jerking the reins of their horses so hard that the animals kicked their front feet high in the air, they averted the first charge of the two nearest Hessians. Then, shouting at the top of their lungs, David and Joseph charged their mounts straight ahead through several more red-coated soldiers, bowling over one of them as they broke through the ranks. Suddenly the moon's bright rays faded as a thick, dark cloud caused a life-saving blackness to envelop the entire ugly scene.

Carefully now, David guided his horse between thickets and trees until most of the sounds of battle were behind him. Joseph, who rejoined the chaplain the following morning, was nowhere to be seen as David noted a line of Continentals to his right fire point-blank into a crowd of Hessians. He took a deep breath and reentered the battle area, gathering up several bewildered Americans and making his way out once more. Gradually some semblance of order was restored by the officers of the retreating Americans as they made a stand against the charges of the British. Without heavy weapons or bullets, the redcoats soon rejoined the main body of their army who were even then marching toward Washington's main body. Sullen American officers moved among angry soldiers counting the wounded and missing.

David was beside himself with a rage that would not abate. Having been a victim of a ferocious night attack, he would never forget nor forgive the British bayoneting of sick, sleeping, and unarmed men. Now, without medical supplies or assistants, with his sick men slain and his nerves shattered, he rode away from the retreating troops to a clump of trees. In the darkness he flung himself to the ground, flailing his fists against the muddy turf. The British were marching unmolested toward his home, while every battle in which he engaged had ended in disaster. "Why, God? Why?" he shouted into the night. His shoulders heaved as uncontrolled weeping engulfed him. In a few moments he mounted his horse, gritted his teeth, and rejoined the men, now trudging the darkened road in retreat.

As Washington attempted to follow Howe, supposing the British general wished to meet him in battle, the British feinted a further movement northwest and then marched hard toward Philadelphia. The Americans now found the British between themselves and the capital. Howe marched in uncontested on September 25. Washington had not performed well by accepted military standards in the campaign of 1777. Outflanked and badly mauled at Brandywine, he narrowly escaped the annihilation of his army. Stymied at Whitemarsh, defeated at Paoli, and outmaneuvered in his attempt to protect Philadelphia, he had lost every objective he had determined to achieve. One of his faults, however, was not a lack of aggressiveness. He had proven that fact in crossing the Delaware the year before when his cause appeared hopeless. General Howe should have remembered that aspect of Washington's character, for whatever else his weaknesses, Washington did not hesitate to fight when the smallest opportunity for success was present. When Howe left only a part of his garrison at Germantown, five miles north of Philadelphia, Washington saw an occasion for a quick and unexpected victory. With Howe retiring to the capital with thoughts of a comfortable winter, Washington sent eleven thousand men in four columns against Germantown on the foggy morning of October 4.

Having cared for the wounded and having buried the dead at Paoli, David was assigned to one of the columns of regulars attacking the center of the British position. Militia units were ordered to turn the British flanks, and with surprising speed, David's troops crashed through the enemy light infantry. After the first volley, the regulars charged with bayonets. They screamed "Revenge Wayne's Affair," and "Remember Paoli," references to the earlier night attack on Wayne's troops at Paoli. David was armed only with a large black leather satchel containing bandages, salves, ointments, and small casks of water. As men fell under bullets and bayonets, David rushed to their sides in a quick attempt to stop the bleeding and set shattered limbs.

Caring first for the fallen Continental soldiers, he also aided the British wounded and dying. As a signal to the stretcher bearers who followed him, David turned the wounded on their backs and placed white cotton bandages somewhere on their uniforms. The dead were turned face down. It would have been a macabre scene for a casual observer, but with the earsplitting sounds of cannon, muskets, rifles, rushing feet, screams, and groans, David's only concern was to minister to as many men as he could and try to keep up with the hard-charging troops.

The heavy fog of early morning may have been the undoing of an apparent American victory, for when the reserves were brought in to reinforce Wayne's column, now driving back the center of the main line, confusion set in. Several British soldiers took refuge in a stone house as the initial thrust of Americans rushed by. Those men now fired on the brigade of reserves moving to the front, who mistook them for a much larger force. Stopping to give battle to a mere handful, the reserves never reached Wayne. When a detachment was left at the house, the main body pushed on toward the major fight. Howe had already given up the battle as lost when the American reserves began firing on Wayne's troops from the rear, supposing they were the British. The thickening fog and firing to his rear forced Wayne to cease his assault, and he eventually withdrew. A golden opportunity was lost that early morning. David, caught in the middle of the firing, rushed to the aid of General Wayne, who was shot. He quickly bandaged the bleeding wound in the commander's foot, and both men went on with their duties. The only thing remaining to be done was to withdraw.

From October 4 to December 1, Washington's army encamped in a strong position at Whitemarsh Church, three miles north of Germantown. When Howe declined to attack, another more pressing menace had to be faced. Snow had fallen and the cold winter descended on an ill-equipped army. While the army had marched hundreds of miles in the past three months, most of their blankets had been discarded as extra weight. Since both armies had purchased and foraged for equipment, the countryside lay stripped of the necessities with which to supply the American army. The British army occupied Philadelphia, using its food, clothing, and shelter. For the Americans, there was practically no supply. David noted that hundreds of the soldiers had no shoes. He devised a method of wrapping their feet with bandages and coating the cotton with mud for warmth, but the few remaining bandages were soon gone as the cold torment grew in the ranks. The only good news was that the American army under Gates had captured the entire northern British army moving down from Canada.

5

Stalemate and Victory

News of victory in Canada did not halt the frigid winter from descending on Washington's decimated army in Pennsylvania, however. On December 1, the army marched across the Schuylkill River to encamp for the winter at a place called Valley Forge. A Quaker, Isaac Potts, had established a forge there years earlier for supplying the region with iron, and thus had given a name to the narrow valley. The army camped on both sides of the hills by the southern bank of the Schuylkill, less than two miles from David's church, and only four miles from his home. The trail to Valley Forge was a trial for those without shoes, as the ground was frozen and full of sharp rocks and bits of iron ore that cut and tore the feet of the marching men, leaving the few long bare spots marked with blood. Washington later wrote: "You might have tracked the army from Whitemarsh to Valley Forge by the blood of their feet."

Slightly over eleven thousand men reached the encampment, but almost three thousand were unfit for duty due to battle wounds or because they had been unable to withstand the nineteen-mile march over the snow-crusted knobs of the wind-swept ridges. It was to these three thousand men that David gave himself in an unstinting effort to relieve their suffering.

Hundreds of the able-bodied men began at once to cut the trees of the surrounding forest. Small log huts approximately twelve feet long by ten feet wide were hastily constructed. The chimneys were build of sticks and mud, the roofs were made of split board puncheons, and the sides were unfinished logs. Between the logs, the cracks were stuffed with moss, mud, and bark, but in spite of their work, the wind whistled through many a crevice to chill the sick soldiers to the point of death. Usually ten to twelve men lived in the crude cabins without floors or beds, and with not even one blanket, on the average, to the hut. The men lay on the ground with

their bare feet toward the fire as they attempted to sleep, while their bodies shivered through the long nights. When the temperatures dropped to extremely low degrees, they sat hunched around a fire built in the center of the hut, since they were unable to endure the cold when stretched out. Sleep was practically impossible in such a position.

David's task with the sick and wounded was almost insuperable. Food was so scarce that they were often without meat for days at a time, and sometimes without flour for longer periods. Smoke mixed with the smell of dirty, perspiring bodies of feverish men made the stench of the small huts indescribable. Lice and bedbugs were customary irritants to other ailments of the men in the medical huts. Often men crawled outside for a breath of fresh air and froze to death in minutes. Many in the huts shed their clothes to rid themselves of the crawling vermin, and they, too, succumbed to the bitter Pennsylvania winter. David sometimes spent half his time in ministering to the sick and the other half in preaching funeral services. More than once, this hardened campaigner excused himself from cleaning oozing wounds to step outside and vomit.

Still, they were an unconquered, if badly mauled, army. Thus, on December 17, 1777, the Continental Congress, now residing in

York, Pennsylvania, proclaimed a day of thanksgiving for the continued existence of the infant United States of America. Washington ordered the entire army to unite in a "devout service" at Valley Forge on the appointed day. David participated in the service on the frozen hillside overlooking the Schuylkill by reading Scripture and leading the shivering congregation in prayer. Both before and after the service, he conducted brief funeral services with other chaplains for four former comrades-in-arms. Afterwards, two nearby civilian doctors were enlisted to care for the sick, and since David was well-known in the area, he was given leave to go home and attempt to round up desperately needed supplies.

Ann hardly recognized the gaunt, bony rider as her husband when David rode up to the house. He was too tired to smile as he dismounted slowly. Ann rushed to his side in a tearful, gloriously happy reunion.

"Oh, David. Oh, David. Oh, David, I love you. I love you, David."

They stood holding one another as soft flakes of snow fell on them and on the children who rushed to their daddy's side.

"Are you all right? Were you wounded at Paoli? Germantown? Please come in out of the cold! Oh, David, we missed you! Are you ill? Are you hungry?"

"Yes," he answered the last question quickly before she rattled off a dozen more. After a hot meal beside the fireplace, David leaned back and surveyed the clean rooms and felt unusually at peace with all around him. The children were in bed after a happy evening with their father.

"Now tell me, Anniefach, how have the children been, and the farm?"

"David, did you know the British were here?"

"Here?" He sat up with a start.

"Yes, here at the farm."

"Dear God! What happened?"

She related how a mounted British patrol had appeared at the house without warning in late September. They were polite, she said, but they demanded that she and the children bring all the men's clothing in the house along with fresh meat and flour. While they were gathering those items, some of the soldiers took their last two horses and all the cows, with the exception of one milk cow and her heifer. When Ann protested, the officer wrote out a receipt for the two horses saying her husband would be repaid by the British quartermaster if he appeared in person. He laughed at her in a mocking tone, knowing that her husband was a part of the patriot army.

"Did they harm any of you?"

"No, not at all. I didn't take a step away from Eleanor, though. She was petrified with fear as the soldiers watched her. I guess I must have glared at the officer so that he knew I was ready to fight to protect her if need be. He finally said, 'No one's going to harm you ladies.'"

David leaned his head on his hands as he vicariously shared their moments of fear.

"I'm so sorry, Annie," he said. They were silent for a few minutes.

"Do you realize that some of those dirty scoundrels are wearing my clothes as underwear when my own men are freezing to death? Ann, it's almost impossible for me not to hate them right into hell."

"I know," she said gently.

Ann related that they had also robbed the church of the Communion service, along with the baptismal robes and sexton's digging tools. David brought greetings from Ann's brother, John, who was serving with the New Jersey militia. They had met after Brandywine and shared a tent for most of the autumn and early winter. The church continued to meet, Ann said. Would he be able to remain until Sunday and preach for them?

"No, Annie, I'm sorry, but I just can't. I must round up all the supplies I can and get back to camp. Anything, believe me, anything I can bring back will save some lives there."

The next morning David repaired an old wagon and hitched his own horse to it. Accompanied by Ann, he loaded every blanket, sheet, and item of food that could be spared and went from house to house gathering up supplies that the neighbors were willing to give. The suffering of the sick and hungry soldiers was common knowledge in the community, but willing farmers were simply unable to provide much to relieve those needs. Some of the farm families were in desperate need themselves, having been stripped to the bare necessities by the invading British. David spent one more night at home and then drove his wagon and goods back to the misery, hunger, and suffering of the American army's winter quarters.

A Connecticut surgeon and contemporary of David's, Dr.

Albigence Waldo, wrote that he "lay cold and uncomfortable last night—my eyes are started out of their orbits like a rabbit's eyes, occasioned by a great cold and smoke. . . . The Lord send that our Commissary of Purchase may live on Fire Cake and water 'till his glutted guts be turned to pasteboard." A growing bureaucracy hindered the arrival of supplies almost as severely as the dearth of available supplies in the immediate region.

When food supplies were at their lowest, officers began eating in rotation on succeeding days from senior to junior officers, including staff chaplains. The desperate privations of officers and men began to meld a spirit of cohesion and comradeship, however, that the Continental army had not experienced previously. General Nathaniel Greene was appointed as supply officer for the army, and almost immediately the situation began to improve. Sending out armed foraging parties with orders to obtain whatever food was available, those detachments began reporting several times each week with fresh supplies.

With improving conditions, David frequently obtained permission to ride home, often taking seriously ill men to recuperate under the care of Ann's clean home and excellent cooking. In January, he drove a wagon home loaded with a desperately sick soldier who suffered lung congestion and deep coughing. Leaving him in Ann's care, and with a good night's sleep, David drove the wagon back toward camp. At White Horse Inn on the Philadelphia Road, he decided to stop and warm himself before continuing on through the cold night. He noticed several horses and a wagon tied to the rail as he entered and warmed himself. In a few minutes, another rider dismounted and entered. The latecomer spoke to the innkeeper.

"Excuse me, sir. Can you direct me to the Germantown Road? I seem to have lost my way."

David stiffened to complete alertness. That accent was like that of no American from these parts, and no one would be inquiring about going to Germantown unless . . . unless he were British. American soldiers would not be that far from their camp. David turned slowly and observed the man. Dressed in civilian clothes, he gave no physical clue of being a British soldier or spy, but David took no chances. As the innkeeper began giving instructions to the stranger, David quietly slipped out a side door and walked to the man's horse. There he found a British saddle and the pack containing the red uniform of a captain of dragoons. His calm disappeared in a flash.

David's anger could be quick and vicious, often pushing him past the boiling point. "Men like these have killed my friends, stolen my property, bayoneted sick men, and terrorized my family. I'll punish him! If he resists, I'll kill him, so help me God!" His thoughts raced on in a torrent of hate. He strode quickly to his wagon, uncovered his pistol, loaded it carefully, concealed it behind his back, and reentered the inn.

"I understand you have lost your way?" David said warmly.

"Why, yes, but I, ah, I believe this kind gentleman has directed me most effectively, and I think I'll be going. But thank you, anyway."

"Allow me to introduce myself." David whipped the pistol from behind him and shoved it deep into the man's stomach. The dragoon's smile was swept away by a look of stark terror.

"My name is David Jones, Captain, and I'm one of those you call a rebel." As he spoke, David's anger mounted. He wished for the man to move, even slightly.

"Not long ago some British rascals like yourself rode to my home back there, stole my cattle, and terrorized my wife and fourteen-year-old daughter. Were you with them?"

"No, sir," the voice was but a whisper.

"I said, were you there?" David shouted and pushed the pistol deeper into the man's abdomen.

"No, sir," the dragoon's voice was louder and his eyes wider.

"Captain, if you'd care to move or try to escape, I'd like the pleasure of blowing your innards against the bar. How about it, Britisher?"

"No, sir, I am your prisoner."

"Then get out and get in my wagon. You're going to headquarters, but it's going to be my headquarters. If you care to try anything brave, I'll kill you."

David tied the captain's horse behind the wagon and ordered the dragoon to drive. Kneeling behind the Englishman, David periodically poked the pistol into his prisoner's ribs to remind him of his presence.

"Halt and identify yourself." The sentries took cover as the wagon neared the camp.

"Chaplain Jones, Fourth Pennsylvania, with a prisoner."

"*CHAPLAIN* Jones?" the dragoon said as he shook his head incredulously, turning to look at David.

"Come in, Chaplain. Who've you got there?" the two sentries asked and looked closely at the dragoon. David pitched the red uniform toward them.

"He was hiding in civilian clothes back at the inn. I'm taking him to headquarters."

Howls of laughter from the sentries followed as David ordered the dragoon to move on. The news of the capture was relayed by voice to headquarters before David arrived. Generals Wayne, Muhlenberg, and Woodward were waiting on the porch of Washington's quarters when the wagon wheels rolled to a stop. Two guards ushered the prisoner away as Wayne broke into laughter.

"Chaplain, you really did it. I wouldn't have believed it unless I saw it with my own eyes. We sent you out for supplies, and you bring back food, bedding, and prisoners. General Washington ought to make you a cavalryman. I haven't had a cavalry officer bring in a prisoner since we got here."

His continued laughter embarrassed David.

"Will that be all, sir?"

"Oh, yes, that's all, David," he said as he tried to control his guffaws. "And good work, David, good work." His mirth subsided to mere chuckles as he walked off with the other generals.

David's admiration for the leadership of the army grew during the trying days of that winter. He was invited often to dine with the general staff, offering thanks for their meager fare. The arrival of drillmaster Von Steuben, the sharp wit of Alexander Hamilton, and the forcefulness of his own commander, General Wayne, made those visits enjoyable amidst the backdrop of such suffering. General Washington was gracious in his thanks to David for his spiritual mien among the staff as well as for his continued services in supplying the sick with goods from his own household. Sitting before a fire with the commander in chief after dinner one evening, the men's conversation turned to the efforts of both armies to gain secret information from the other.

"Doctor, do your family and friends report seeing many strangers in civilian clothes in the area?"

"Oh, yes, General Washington. All the folk have become highly suspicious of any stranger since they can't always tell whether he is British or one of us."

"Do you think the dragoon you took prisoner was a spy?"

"No, I don't think so, sir. As you know, our own men ride alone to one of our distant units in civilian clothes just to keep from being noticed. But they are on strict military business. I think he was just lost, that's all."

"Hmmm. Well, I'm still quite interested in this business, Doctor Jones. I would appreciate your communicating anything you hear of this directly to me in the future. Would you do that, please?"

"That I will do, sir. You can count on it."

David thought over that conversation often in the next few weeks, wondering why the commander did not wish for David to go through proper channels with such information. Was there an informer on the staff? Was there someone he did not trust? He never knew, but he did keep Washington personally informed of strangers he encountered while on supply and preaching missions as well as occasional trips home.

The Baptist churches in the area, anxious for news from their associates in the American camp, often invited David to preach. Since many of the churches were in close proximity to British camps, care had to be exercised lest David become a prisoner. Still, he enjoyed preaching his "Ticonderoga Sermon," condemning the British and pleading with the patriots to keep their courage. When he preached at the Pennepack church, he had to spend the evening with a church member on Saturday night and walk by British sentries in the midst of two other families on his way to the Sunday service. It didn't take long for the enemy to learn that the loss of one of their officers to an American chaplain might be connected to a chaplain preaching "sedition" to Baptist churches right under their watchful eyes. Orders for David's arrest were issued from General Howe's headquarters.

Pastor William Miller had served the Methodist church west of Philadelphia for only a short time when the war came to Pennsylvania. Tall and slender, he had long black hair pulled behind his head and tied with a small ribbon. Though he had remained neutral through the early stages of the war, it was his misfortune to have a sick parishioner in Chester County on the day a British cavalry patrol was sent to watch for and arrest David. Leisurely riding along toward a home less than two miles beyond the Jones' farm, he was startled by a patrol that suddenly surrounded him with drawn pistols.

"Halt, Reverend. You're under arrest."

"What?"

"Dismount, sir. Search him."

Miller was thoroughly frightened and dismayed. He was searched and found to have nothing more incriminating than a Bible, held up for the officer to see.

"Why are you arresting me?"

"Well, to list only a few things: being a member of the rebel army, appearing in civilian clothes as a spy, arresting one of our officers, stealing supplies, and preaching sedition, rebellion, and revolution in every Baptist church in this countryside. How's that?"

"That's nonsense, sir. I am William Miller from the Methodist church on Lancaster Road. I've never been in the rebel army, and I certainly don't go around preaching in Baptist churches."

"You're a minister, aren't you?"

"Well, yes, but . . ."

"And you're riding to your home up there, aren't you, Jones?"

"My name is not Jones, and I live a good six miles east of here."

"Now, now, Jones. Ministers aren't supposed to lie, now, are they? You just get back on your horse and come with us."

It didn't take long for the British to realize their mistake, and news of the arrest quickly reached the members of David's church. A rider was sent dashing off to the farm to warn Ann and the children while another rider headed for the camp at Valley Forge. David received the news as he was hitching up a wagon for yet another supply expedition home.

His disappointment was keen, as this obviously meant that it was unsafe to go out of camp as long as the British were nearby. Yet he felt a touch of pride as the news was circulated that the Reverend Doctor Jones had been singled out by the enemy for capture. Still, he was bitter over not being able to go home to his family, so close and yet so far. The bitterness escaped momentarily when he heard about Reverend Miller.

"Well, if somebody had to be denied preaching for a while yesterday, I guess it's good it was the Methodists," he said as he unhitched the wagon. "They don't get much, anyway." He was not smiling.

General Greene's energetic leadership in supplying the camp with food and clothes, coupled with Von Steuben's new drilling methods, increased the tempo at Valley Forge as activity of the troops corresponded with the arrival of spring in eastern Pennsylvania. Unexpectedly, a large run of shad in the Delaware River permitted the troops to feast on fish for a two-week period in April. Troops on leave began returning for duty as enlistments increased daily. After shrinking to a mere four thousand effectives in the winter, Washington's army soon numbered slightly more than thirteen thousand, many of them hardened campaigners anxious to have another chance at the invaders. On May 6, 1778, the Continental army celebrated its greatest day of jubilation as a military review was held. Nearby families were invited to tables of food while a band played, and an army, still poorly clad, wheeled its columns in perfect order, grounded it arms with a crash, and performed its recent lessons without a blunder.

While enthusiasm mounted at Valley Forge after the survival of a bitter winter, one other factor stood out as the greatest blessing the young nation had yet known; France and Spain had entered the war with America against Great Britain! As a result of the tremendous victory of Gates over Burgoyne at Saratoga, New York, and the ability of Washington to survive in the face of Howe's experienced troops, the French and Spanish decided to throw in their lot with those in revolt against their long-standing enemy. A magnificent French fleet, a large contingent of infantry, and desperately needed supplies were even now on their way from France and Spain. The British in Philadelphia were now in a tight tactical fix. To be hemmed in by Washington on one side and a powerful French force moving up the Delaware on the other was to court disaster. When British commissioners offering conciliatory acts to the rebels on June 4 were turned away, the redcoats had no other choice but to flee to New York across New Jersey.

As Washington's army prepared to move out to intercept General Clinton, now in command of the British army, David received orders on June 18 to remain at Valley Forge with the sick. He was upset and angry that he could not play an active role in the final battles he felt were approaching. Yet no amount of appeal would change General Wayne's personnel decisions. Wayne spoke to David in fast, clipped tones as his chaplain came to appeal the order.

"You know the situation here. You, alone, of all the doctors are trusted by the people in this valley and can therefore obtain supplies. We have an adequate contingent of combat doctors now. You have had your share of fighting and then some. No, David, I will not transfer you to the advance unit. You are in charge of the medical detachment here. Good luck. That is all."

Wayne walked away without further word as his infantry began marching on a path that would parallel Clinton's flight across New Jersey. David angrily kicked the dirt in front of the tent. He did not accept disappointment easily. His own troops were headed out toward the Hopewell area he knew so well, while the thought of a long summer in the misery of those smoky, stinking huts after the agonizing winter was almost more than he could bear. Somehow, the thought of being home often, preaching at his church, and long nights of restful sleep did not comfort him at the moment. The overwhelming desire to be a part of an enthusiastic, moving body of comrades-in-arms anticipating battle shut out the disadvantages accompanying fighting armies: the weary marches, the hunger, the pain, the death. David was not now, and never would be, acclimated to routine work. His greatest effectiveness came in bursts of activity as he moved quickly from one thing to another. He needed a multiplicity of challenges. He desired a greater foe to fight than sniffles, influenza, stubbed toes, and lice. He shook his head sadly and walked to the huts at the top of the hill.

News from the army brought reports of their camping at Hopewell while Clinton passed through Crosswicks. Then a great battle occurred just outside Freehold where the British continued the retreat. After the battle, Clinton marched his troops through Middletown and on to Sandy Hook. David had lived and labored at all those places. Fears for the safety of the Stillwells and other church friends made waiting for additional news agonizingly long. He spent several nights at home each week, as the work at camp was light, and he preached almost every Sunday in the Baptist churches of the area. Even though he was considered something of a celebrity in the area, his attention was constantly drawn toward the northeast and the moving American army. On August 8, David received the long-awaited message: "Report to the Second Brigade, Fourth Pennsylvania at Morristown."

Following another hurried farewell with his family, David joined his unit to find that the British were blockaded in New York by ships under the French Admiral D'Estaing, who was supporting Washington's troops. The remainder of 1778 quietly slipped into occasional raids and intrigues, and then, unfortunately, into miserable, unequipped winter quarters. This winter, however, David was more experienced in how to treat the sick in the small log houses that dotted the heights above Morristown. In addition, he had an adequate supply of bedding, bandages, and medicines.

Though army winter quarters would have been uncomfortable anywhere, at least he was in a far superior position to the Valley Forge days of the previous winter. One thing the army still lacked, however, was adequate clothing. General Wayne wrote the Pennsylvania Assembly that they were "half naked while reports reach us of idleness, dissipation, and extravagance in Philadelphia." The Continental paper money was depreciating daily as the officers watched morale sink to ever lower ebbs.

Wayne experienced problems on every hand as Major General St. Clair was placed in command of the Pennsylvania Line, passing over Wayne. This political shifting, with the shortage of supplies, brought Wayne to the Assembly to plead his case. He wrung from them half pay for his soldiers for life, suitable uniforms, and exemption from taxation of the land grants that had been made to them. However, the action did not become final until March when winter had spent itself and the suffering was eased with the return of spring. He received no satisfaction concerning his command, and so he asked to "return to domestic life, and leave the blustering field of Mars to the possession of gentlemen of more worth." In February, he returned home.

Deep depression settled on David at Morristown as the high hopes of the previous spring, when the army pursued Clinton to New York, had given way to petty bickering, political machinations, continued lack of supplies, and now to the loss of his friend and commander, General Wayne. Victory, which had seemed so imminent just a few months earlier, now appeared to be forever out of reach. Enlisted men refused to take orders; few appeared for religious services; and desertions mounted. David asked for a brief leave and was refused. He became sullen and perfunctory in his duties as neither he nor anyone else nearby seemed to take note of a possible offensive being planned by the general staff.

General Clinton's strategy was to lure Washington away from New Jersey, hoping that the British could march unmolested back to Pennsylvania, thus pinching Washington between the two British armies. When sporadic, yet vicious, attacks of the Connecticut coastal towns failed to lure Washington across the Hudson to their defense, Clinton sent half of his force northward, taking Stony and Verplanck's points. Washington was tempted to move up the Hudson and attack a force of nearly equal size, but the British in New York City would be in Philadelphia before he could return. He prudently remained at Middlebrook, where he had moved from Morristown. Another plan of operation involved that aggressive fighting officer, Anthony Wayne.

On June 21, 1779, Washington wrote to Wayne asking him to rejoin the army and take command of a new, small, light infantry unit being organized for a secret mission. One thousand three hundred fifty picked troops were to take Stony Point in a swift move, with the main body of Washington's army continuing to hold Clinton in New York. The planning and training were to be accomplished in thirty days. David asked for and was granted permission to be assigned as the unit's temporary chaplain. Wayne requested "fine uniforms," books of tactics for his officers, and a large supply of "espontoons," a broad-bladed, keen-pointed spear. He did not receive the uniforms or books, but the spears arrived in time for instruction in how to use them in a charge. This was to be no gentlemanly assault or textbook example of military drill. "Remember the Paoli Affair" was on the soldiers' lips as they prepared for the attack.

Stony Point was a high spike of land, virtually an island, thrusting itself into the Hudson River from the west bank. It commanded the river with its cannons, forbidding any movement of enemy ships upstream or downstream. In all but the driest seasons, a fifty-yard-wide moat of water separated the Point from land. A frontal attack could be defended easily by a small garrison, and the British had a sizable force there. Preparing his troops downriver at Sandy Beach, a frontal assault was contemplated by Washington. Wayne advised against it, but added, "General, I'll storm hell, if you will plan it." When Washington at last left the details to Wayne, the Pennsylvanian issued the following instructions: the attack would come at night; spears and bayonets would be used in order to insure secrecy; the first men to enter the enemy's works would receive $500, $400, $300, $200, and $100; and they would round up civilians as temporary prisoners while they moved forward. There would not be a repeat of the Tory treachery at Paoli, for in addition to taking civilians as prisoners, a patrol was being sent out to kill all dogs within a three-mile radius, lest their barking give an untimely warning.

All noncombatants remained at Sandy Beach, including David, as the troops marched away at noon, July 15, 1779. David preached to the men only once on a Sunday morning during their month-long training, but he felt a personal pride in the men as they disappeared in the forest. Marching along a deer track, they arrested a "Widow Calhoun" who was on her way to the British with chickens and greens. Her howls of protest were quickly silenced by Wayne, who told Captain McLane to "cut out that old harridan's tongue if she yelps one more time." Wayne's countenance and demeanor before a battle were fierce, defying all contradiction and dispute. That he was deadly serious was apparent. Widow Calhoun shrunk into frightened silence.

At midnight, the troops entered the causeway waist deep in water. Halfway across the sandbar on the opposite side, a sentry was aroused and fired his musket. As they charged up the hill, a volley killed several Continentals instantly, and a bullet grazed General Wayne's head, knocking him flat. Screaming from the ground, he commanded them to charge. Cold steel pushed on through the startled British, who fled in panic toward the highest point. Wayne regained his feet and his bearings as his soldiers leaped among the British. When he arrived at the top and heard cries of "Mercy!" "Quarter!" he stopped the slaughter instantly.

While David helped with the wounded for several days, the victory was greeted with great celebration at Sandy Beach and Middlebrook. The British strategy was foiled; American spirits were revived; and Wayne was returned to duty with a tremendous victory to his credit. David was overjoyed at the sudden turn of events as a new, though brief, enthusiasm returned to the American cause. Gold medals were struck by Congress and presented to Wayne and his men to commemorate the victory, but when the commander begged for shoes for his men, no supplies were forthcoming. Congress could provide gold medals, but not shoes, a fact not lost on the barefoot soldiers. In December, the Virginians in Wayne's command were ordered to their home state to fight in the southern campaign. When they left New Jersey in the bitter cold of winter, dozens of the soldiers piled on individual wagons because of the lack of shoes for the flower of American infantry.

Another long, hard winter lay in store for the weary Continental army. If Washington was less than pleased with the meager results of 1779, General Clinton was most unhappy as well. Promised reinforcements sailed into New York harbor in August, but only half the number expected arrived, bringing with them a contagious fever. With Stony Point lost and his troops bottled up in New York, Clinton became enamored with war in the south. The New York-New Jersey theater of military action, therefore, grew very quiet during the winter of 1779–1780. David took leave in January and spent a busy three months preaching in Pennsylvania and New Jersey Baptist churches denied to him by the earlier British occupation.

He enjoyed his brief visit home, although Ann became increasingly irritable as David rode off to various churches for days at a time. Five-year-old David was obviously afflicted with a chronic and major illness. He was so thin as to frighten his father on David's return from the latest campaign. Even the heaviest starch diet added no weight or strength to his frail little arms and legs. He was much smaller than other children of his age, and his constant fever and coughing caused Ann to miss many nights of sleep. Their farm was productive; they harvested a good vegetable garden and a large crop of corn. It was extremely difficult, however, for Ann to be mother, father, farmer, nurse, and church member. David's salary from the army was practically worthless due to the great depreciation of Continental currency, and what little savings they had were long since spent. The British had taken their cattle and horses.

"Must you go to Delaware, David?" Ann asked.

"You know very well that the Welsh Tract has invited several other churches in to hear me bring a firsthand report of the war and to preach to them." He was irritated that she would question his going.

"Yes, I know of their need for you, but I also know all too well that your family needs you, too. I don't know how much longer I can keep up this pace, David, and I'm so worried about young David, I don't know what to do."

"I'm sorry, Ann. I've done all I know how to do for Davey. Do you want me to try to find Dr. Shipley and see if he can treat him?"

"No, no other doctor can do more for him than you have. The truth is, I just want you here with us when you can be." She began crying, but he did not go to her.

"Ann, I know it isn't any easier being a minister's wife than it is to be a minister. Would you like for me to send word that I won't come because my wife is upset with me for being gone so much in the army?"

"Oh, of course not."

"Well, why don't you make this as pleasant as possible, then?"

"I know you have your own set of problems, but, David, you surely understand that. . . . Oh, forget it."

She continued pressing the cuffs of one of his white shirts with a waffled iron. He paused for a moment, looked at her intently, and then went to his room to continue packing.

The rounds of preaching and helping at home came to an end on March 1, 1780. David reported to his brigade, where he spent more time with his chaplain's duties than with the medical work. Preaching opportunities were more frequent due to the static condition of the army. The British continued to remain in New York with Washington's army and Admiral D'Estaing's fleet maintaining an effective blockade. David volunteered for duty on several foraging expeditions as a medical aide, but for the most part was content to preach, assist the doctors, and visit the churches in the area of northern New Jersey and southern New York. Active fighting had given way to that most dreaded of all diseases to David—routine.

David's routine, as well as the routine of all other patriotic Americans, came to a decisive halt with the shocking discovery of the Benedict Arnold scandal. General Arnold had proven himself earlier as a capable and sometimes brilliant officer with the American army, and the news of his changing allegiance to the British was, therefore, completely unexpected to those who knew him. Arnold was in command at West Point when he entered into a conspiracy with General Clinton to surrender the post, assume a command in the British army, and be rewarded with six thousand British pounds sterling. As General Washington was in the vicinity of West Point when the plot was near fruition, he almost became the largest pawn in the tragic scene.

No one was more surprised, shocked, or disappointed with the treacherous Benedict Arnold scandal than David, and he could not forget his earlier conversations with Washington about spies and intrigue while at Valley Forge. "Perhaps," he wondered to himself, "General Washington may have suspected something like this long ago." Many soldiers of the ranks had previously deserted to the enemy. Soldiers destitute of food and clothing, devoid of emotional and educational stability, and fearful for their families' well-being and penniless condition had gone over to the British for their secure sterling pounds. Yet their acts were quickly forgotten by all but their most intimate former friends.

Now, however, a bonafide American hero had changed his Continental purple for the red coat of the invading enemy. For an infant country desperately in need of heroes, Arnold's treason was a heavy shock. His unforgiveable sin to his American contemporaries was that he robbed them of a hero. It was precisely because of his previous brilliant performance that the name of Benedict Arnold became synonymous with treachery, treason, and disloyalty.

The conspiracy failed, however, when Major John Andre, a talented young officer sent by Clinton to settle the details with Arnold, was captured. Wearing civilian clothes, he was held briefly as a spy. Washington and his generals offered to exchange Andre for Arnold, but when Clinton refused, the major was hanged. Other attempts to bribe American officers and congressional officials were attempted by Clinton, but each failed in bitter reaction to Arnold's contemptuous action. The British could not gain by bribery what they could not do by force. Clinton's effectiveness in the northern theater had come to an inglorious end.

When Arnold's deceit became known on September 25, 1780, David was with Wayne's brigade at Tappan, New York, below Nyack, stationed with General William Irvine's Second Pennsylvanians. At one o'clock in the morning of the twenty-sixth, a rider arrived at Wayne's and Irvine's headquarters bringing the news and ordering the two brigades to march to West Point immediately. A large British contingent was marching north to occupy the fort, expecting it to be handed over by Arnold. Since the loss of that post would imperil Washington's entire army, the men hastily assembled in the dark of night, were issued short rations, and marched away in the blackness surrounding Haverstraw Creek. David rode up and down the line of marching men offering encouragement, treating blistered feet, and sharing his horse with weary men. In four hours, on a dark night, without a single halt or man left behind, they arrived at the pass at Haverstraw Landing. Their presence was announced to the commander at West Point, and that post was happily secure once again.

Discontent was not restricted to those in high places, however. In the south, where the war was waxing hot with feverish activity, the soldiers had little time to be concerned with pay and uniforms. In that area, men were defending homes and families, while in the north the fighting had deteriorated to a blockade of New York and an occasional foray by small units. When Washington's northern army had been fighting on Long Island, retreating across New Jersey, and defending Philadelphia, the soldiers had been fighting to preserve their lives and property just as the southern army was doing in the winter of 1780–1781. Now, however, with military activity diminished, the northern troops began to sense that their own personal problems and a list of the failures of Congress and their state assemblies was beginning to grow longer. Leaders then appeared to make those private lists of grievances causes for discontent and, at last, for open rebellion.

Some men of the Pennsylvania Line had served with the army since 1775, a total of five years by the end of 1780. For their efforts in withstanding a superior British army during that period, they had suffered unspeakable hardships. Food and clothing were so scarce each winter that the death rate was exorbitant. The production of shoes, particularly, had been almost nonexistent during the past five years. Men watched their friends die of malnutrition due to the steady diet of a little flour and greasy pork. While the British dined and danced in warm Philadelphia and New York ballrooms, well supplied by their powerful navy, the Continental army trembled in the cold, starved, and died in crude, smoke-filled huts on frozen hillsides. The Continental currency used to pay the troops was so worthless that some soldiers started fires with the paper money. On March 1, 1780, nearly $200 million in Continental money was in circulation, but Congress estimated that forty Continental dollars were worth only one of the Spanish dollars upon which they were modeled. Over the winter of 1780–1781, the currency lost almost all value except as a souvenir. Then laws were passed requiring that cheap, worthless paper be accepted as legal tender. Tories contributed counterfeit bills to the already inflated legal tender. In Philadelphia, a pound of beef sold for several hundred Continental dollars in paper. At last, in the winter, the majority of the Pennsylvania Line could count twelve months since they had been paid a single penny of the wages that were due them.

Desertions had been constant throughout the war as men went home to plough and plant in the spring or to cut firewood for freezing families in the winter. Those desertions increased alarmingly by December, 1780, as the high hopes of victory in 1778 had long since been dashed by the static war in the north and a failing army in the south. Even the entry of the French and Spanish did not bring the anticipated victory. Camp followers were not introduced to the Americans by the French, but the European theatrical productions, dueling, and lives of luxury and pomp among the officer corps did little to help the morale of the Pennsylvania Line. The Marquis de

Lafayette separated his troops, at last, from the Continentals "so that the Americans would not learn the corrupt habits of the French."

David's sermons continually warned of God's judgment on "profaneness and dissolute morals." Wayne and the other generals wrote to their state assemblies pleading for shoes, thread, cloth, and food, but all to little or no avail. More than one soldier and civilian agreed with David's statement in a letter to Ann as he said, "The marvel of this war is not that we have held a fine British army at bay, but that we have kept our own army together." Even more severe storm clouds were gathering within the Continental ranks, however.

The final stroke that pushed the Pennsylvania Line toward ultimate discontent concerned enlistment terms. In the early years of the war, men enlisted for a calendar year, though many wished, even then, for terms to last for the duration of the conflict. Congress finally did expand the terms of service to three years, and for a great host of the Pennsylvanians those three years were to end on December 31, 1780. Men who had suffered through Valley Forge and Morristown winters, been wounded at Monmouth and Stony Point, and starved and been beaten by the elements now looked homeward to families and friends. They had served the cause of independence well; let others take up their ranks now, they reasoned, for they were homeward bound for New Year's Day. When, however, word was passed from hut to hut at Christmas that neither Congress nor the officers were going to allow their enlistments to expire at the appointed date, an ugly growl emanated from the dark and cold camp.

New Year's night found David seated in the staff hut with General Wayne, Colonel Walter Stewart, Major James Grier, Surgeon John Rodgers, and several orderlies. The mood was somber as the men drank lukewarm tea under a faintly glowing lamp.

"General, I'm concerned about the mood of these men. Some of them have been friends of mine for years, and yet they haven't spoken to me for days. I'm not sure what they're up to," David's voice was concerned.

"That's right, sir. Several sickhuts won't even let me in to tend them," said Rodgers.

"How are the other regiments taking the extension of enlistments? Does anyone know?" asked Wayne as he looked toward Colonel Stewart, who had been to Washington's headquarters only the day before.

"Well, sir, no good news has come from any of the camps, but General Washington. . . ."

A strange shuffling noise was heard outside.

"Quiet!" ordered Wayne.

He stepped toward the entrance, and as he did, the door was flung open by a well-dressed Continental sergeant armed with a pistol. The sergeant shoved the weapon against Wayne's chest.

"Back up, sir, or I'll have to kill you."

Several other soldiers dashed into the hut, one pointing a cocked pistol next to David's head. Each of the staff was closely guarded. It happened so quickly that the men had time only to stand and gape in disbelief at the incredulous scene.

"Put those weapons, down," ordered Wayne.

"Shut up, General. We're taking over, and if one of you so much as moves, we will kill him."

"This is mutiny!" Wayne shouted.

"That's right, General, and this mutineer is going to have to shoot you if you don't shut up."

Loud shouts of confusion and running feet were heard as a tumult grew outside the hut. Several officers just outside Wayne's quarters grabbed their sabers and attempted to beat the ranks of mutineers into submission as they approached the headquarters area. A volley from the rebels dropped five of the young officers; three of them were killed instantly.

"Everyone flat on the floor," commanded the sergeant inside the hut. David lay prone on the floor as he felt the barrel of a pistol against the back of his neck. The soldier's knee dug deeply into the small of his back. Outside, the mutineers gained control of four fieldpieces and fired several rounds of grapeshot across the parade ground, clearing out the small line of men assembled on the far side by several loyal officers. The darkness, mercifully, prevented accuracy, and only a few were injured as the rebels gained control of the open drill area. When all fighting had ceased, the rebels assembled in ranks. Thirteen hundred men were readied to march off into the night as another sergeant appeared in Wayne's doorway.

"Let them up now, Sergeant," he said.

"Do you know the penalty for what you're doing, Sergeant?" General Wayne's demeanor was so intense as he arose that the sergeant cautioned him by waving a sword close to his throat.

"Yes, sir, I do. And I also know the penalty for breaking my legal enlistment by extension, and I know the penalty for refusing to pay me, and I know the penalty of having our families starve and freeze when our congressmen are warm and stuffed with food." His eyes flashed as his voice rose.

"We have suffered the same indignities that you have," David's quick retort surprised everyone. The pistol was forced back toward his head.

The noncommissioned officer looked toward David and spoke in less abrasive tones.

"Yes, Chaplain, I know you have, and if we all didn't respect you officers, we would have shot you straightaway. You have been a good general, sir," he looked at Wayne, "and we don't blame you for our destitute condition. We know you, the chaplain, and others have given of your own money and goods and pleaded with the Assembly for us. But since you can't help us, we're going to help ourselves. Now then, we're going to block the doors and windows when we march out of here. If anyone steps out of this hut, he will be shot. I hope nobody does. All right, men, move out."

"Sergeant. . . ."

"Silence, sir!" Wayne's interjection was cut short as the sergeant backed out of the door, shutting it and ordering a wagon pushed against it. The staff heard the commands of several sergeants as the troops moved away from the camp. A stunned silence prevailed in David's hut as the staff paused to collect their wits in the midst of the mind-numbing confusion.

When the sounds of marching feet had faded into the night, Wayne and the others shoved the door open. Riders were sent to Washington's headquarters, and a patrol was ordered to follow the mutineers. Wayne was convinced that the column was headed to join the British at Elizabethtown, but every report that came back indicated that their destination was southwesterly toward Philadelphia. Why were they headed away from both their own army and the British? A note picked up in a deserter's hut told why; they were not going to join the enemy, but rather they were going to capture the Continental Congress at Philadelphia and make their demands good at last. David's sympathy, if not his full approval of their methods, went with them.

"You know, General," he said to Wayne, "when St. Clair retreated from Fort 'Ti,' John Adams said, 'We shall never be able to defend a post till we shoot a general.' Maybe a better statement now is that we shall never be able to maintain the nation till we shoot a few politicians."

"I understand your meaning, David, but you know we can't let them do this thing. Why don't several of you from my staff join me and let's follow them and try to talk some sense into their heads?"

"You're right, sir. I'll go with you. They could certainly use a chaplain now," David spoke up quickly as others volunteered to accompany the commander.

The insurrectionists allowed only General Wayne, Colonels Butler and Stewart, Chaplain Jones, and two orderlies to follow directly behind the marching troops and maintain a daily dialogue with the leaders. Under Wayne's influence, the men elected leaders and maintained an effective and orderly discipline as they marched. The general wisely sent for President Reed of the Pennsylvania Assembly to join him and settle the grievances before the troops reached Philadelphia. Before he arrived, however, two emissaries were sent by British General Clinton to entice the force to join with their former enemies. Pardons, money, increased rank, and food for their families were promised them if they would exchange their shabby garments for the neat and warm British red coats. The mutinous leaders met with Wayne, seeking his advice about how to deal with the messengers from Clinton. On returning from Wayne's camp, the rebels heard the emissaries once again and then pronounced them as spies and sentenced them to be hung. These angry mutineers were not to be trifled with.

Chaplain Jones was invited to accompany the two men to the gallows. Instead of bringing soft words of comfort to dying men, he led them from a tent to the waiting tree reading Scriptures concerning the justice and vengeance of God, all in a loud voice. Biblical passages such as "Vengeance is mine, saith the Lord" were intended for the ears of the rebellious Continental troops more than for the two condemned men. David was not acting the role of the loving shepherd; his was the voice of an angry prophet.

President Reed arrived at Princeton shortly after the executions and agreed to discharge those whose terms of service were concluded, to pay them back pay, to provide some clothing, and to proclaim a general amnesty for their insurrection. Neither Congress nor the Pennsylvania Assembly had been able to relieve the men of their grievances before the revolt. Now, however, when the two groups of politicians learned that thirteen hundred armed men were marching on them to make their demands at the point of the bayonet, means for supplying the unfortunate troops were quickly discovered. When the last men were discharged and paid, two-thirds of the men reenlisted on the spot and marched to Trenton with General Wayne in command. The mutiny was thus concluded with a minimum of debilitating influence on the patriot cause.

In the spring of 1781, it appeared that the war would go on forever, with victory going to the least exhausted of the combatants. Both sides were weary. Great Britain held a few American seaports, but the Continentals controlled the vast countryside. Both treasuries were nearly empty. Reports from the south reaching Washington were conflicting accounts of Lord Cornwallis and his British army moving through the Carolinas with numerous victories and astounding American triumphs at King's Mountain and Cowpens. Cornwallis disliked a prudent defensive war, and thus his taste for the offensive initiative moved him ever northward toward Virginia and infamy. Though American militia units were appearing all around him, and signs of another Burgoyne-Saratoga disaster mounted, he pushed on toward the north. When Admiral de Grasse's French fleet appeared at his back in the Chesapeake Bay and Lafayette opposed him to the front, a golden opportunity was presented to the American cause. Washington and the French General Rochambeau kept enough troops to bottle Clinton up in New York, and then rushed the majority of their troops toward Yorktown, Virginia, where Cornwallis was digging in. A fresh flow of French money and equipment smoothed the American army's march southward.

Part of the Pennsylvania Line was ordered to swing around Cornwallis and reinforce Lafayette's forces before the arrival of Washington and Rochambeau. David accompanied Wayne's troops to York, Pennsylvania, where they rendezvoused with other units. On May 20, 1781, the Pennsylvania Line had formed ranks for the march into Virginia when a number of enlisted men on the right of each regiment began to shout obscenities, calling for the paymaster to pay them in "real and not ideal money." While it was true that the Pennsylvania legislature had fulfilled its promise to pay the men by issuing even more worthless paper money, another mutiny seemed impossible with victory almost within their grasp.

The officers ordered the men into their tents as General Wayne rode to the middle of the line. David watched from the front. Many of the men refused to break ranks, and with that last refusal, General

Wayne drew his saber, dismounted, and rushed the front rank of the dissenters. Cursing wildly, he struck a leader across the chest as other officers attacked the remainder of the protesters. In a moment, the leaders of the revolt were subdued, arrested, and lined up before General Wayne and his staff for a hurried court martial. Wayne was almost beside himself with rage. Determining that two of the men were the prime movers, and that twelve others had followed their lead, Wayne sentenced the two to be hanged immediately with the twelve to erect the ropes and serve as executioners. David could hardly believe what he heard. Never had he seen General Wayne so overwrought. He thought for an instant that the commander had lost his mind.

"I'll give you twelve men thirty minutes to arrange the execution. If you are not prepared by then, you will all be shot. Now get to it. We have a war to fight."

He jerked his head toward David, "Chaplain, see to the condemned men."

David stared hard at his commander and friend to be sure he had heard correctly. Wayne, shaking with rage, jumped to his feet and paced up and down while a suitable place for the hanging was found.

One of the condemned men spoke to David, "Oh, Chaplain, can't you do something? We didn't mean anything 'cept we wanted to be paid. Please, Chaplain, do something, please, please!"

The other condemned man broke into sobs. David's own emotions were on the surface as he looked into the eyes of the pleading man only with great difficulty. David couldn't speak as he shook his head slowly and walked toward his horse and the Bible that was tucked in the saddlebag.

As they walked toward the two ropes hanging from a tree at the edge of the clearing, David did not read of God's justice and wrath, but with a tender heart he read the Twenty-third Psalm. He fought to control the emotion that threatened to choke him. As the small group moved slowly forward, the men spoke above his reading voice.

"Please, Chaplain, speak to the general. He'll listen to you. Calm him down, sir, please. He'll listen to you. Please, Chaplain, please," the first man's voice was desperate.

The second man sobbed and muttered to himself, "I'm sorry. I'm so sorry. Please forgive me, Mary. Forgive me, Christine. Oh, God, I'm so sorry. I'm sorry."

David thought he would faint as the men were hoisted above the ground. Never had he felt more useless, more helpless, of such little value in a moment when God's word was needed. The troops reformed and marched toward Virginia as "Mad Anthony" Wayne rode up and down the line daring any soldier to so much as utter an unnecessary sound. There was a heavy pall of silence as they marched through the night.

Wayne joined Lafayette at Fredericksburg and moved down the peninsula after engaging Cornwallis in a spirited fight. Though badly outnumbered, Wayne charged the best of the British troops, escaping only because the enemy could not believe that a much smaller force was in front of them. David assisted with the wounded for several days following that engagement. The Pennsylvania Line was then transferred to an area between Portsmouth and Petersburg in case Cornwallis tried to escape toward the south from his encirclement at Yorktown. The French and American armies faced the British from the land of the peninsula, and any escape by water was covered by the French fleet. Unless Clinton could reinforce or evacuate Cornwallis soon, the British southern army would be forced to surrender or face annihilation. With ammunition and food supplies depleted, Cornwallis held on while Clinton prepared for movement south. Before he arrived, however, Cornwallis surrendered his entire army on October 17, 1781.

David joined the Pennsylvania Line staff for the surrender ceremonies on the nineteenth in an open field outside Yorktown. With the Americans on the left of the British and the French to their right, the defeated army of Cornwallis marched out and stacked its arms in surrender. David noted that the disparity between the bedraggled victors and the well-dressed vanquished was striking. He also noted that the British displayed much arrogance, and many of the enlisted men were "much in liquor." Not much celebration followed the surrender, as the military men knew that British army contingents still remained in New York and in Charlestown. David ate a hearty evening meal with the staff and then took a night ride on his horse toward Hampton. He was calm and at peace with himself and the world. His thoughts turned back to the many discouragements of the past six years, and he wished for Ann to share the pleasantness of his thoughts. He was happy, contented with a great victory, and desirous of a time of thanksgiving to God. Remembering another night when he rode away from badly mauled troops at Paoli, David dismounted and led his horse into the darkness of a nearby clump of trees. Kneeling on soft moss, he bowed his head and thanked his God for a sustaining power through six difficult, desperate years.

There was still one more campaign facing David, however, before the war would come to an end. Wayne was ordered to South Carolina to reinforce General Nathaniel Greene, who had forced the British into Charlestown. David accompanied the troops to the outskirts of Charlestown where they received fresh orders sending them farther south into Georgia. Since Greene could maintain an effective blockade of Charlestown with his own forces, he sent the Pennsylvanians to deal with the Tory-Indian conspiracy in the vicinity of Savannah. Greene told Wayne, "Try, by every means, to soften the malignity and deadly resentments existing between Whigs and Tories, and put a stop, as much as possible, to the cruel custom of putting people to death after surrender."

On January 12, 1782, David's detachment crossed Sister's Ferry on the Savannah River using canoes for the men, swimming the horses, and leaving the cannon behind. Wayne could count on slightly less than one thousand men to drive out thirteen hundred British regulars, five hundred well-organized Tories, and an indeterminate host of Creek and Cherokee warriors. Establishing himself twenty-five miles upriver from the British headquarters, Wayne stretched a line of temporary outposts twenty miles south to the Ogeechee River, cutting the British lines of communication to the interior. On May 21, the Americans learned that one thousand British soldiers were marching south out of Savannah, and the Pennsylvanians moved out to engage them. May 23 found Wayne's forces within sight of Savannah, where they camped for the night. A large body of Indians led by Chief Guristersijo and a British officer crept around the American camp on the night of June 24.

Shots and shouts awoke David that night as light infantry pickets were driven back into camp by the charging Indians. Hand-to-hand combat broke out all around him as he ran without pistol or sword toward the headquarters tent. He saw General Wayne slashing with his saber from horseback, and then suddenly Wayne and his horse collapsed in a grotesque heap only a few yards from David's feet. Supposing the general mortally wounded, David ran toward him to give what assistance he could. Before he reached the commander, surrounded by gleaming knives, tomahawks, men in death-gripping struggles, and bayonets, Wayne was on his feet organizing the men into a defensive line. Wayne's horse was dead, but the general was unscathed. David picked up a long Indian knife for his own defense if he should be attacked, and once more headed toward the medical unit.

The Pennsylvanians now had an enemy who knew how to use cold steel at close quarters. As the two groups of combatants engaged in violent action for thirty bloody minutes, injured men crawled for cover away from shrieking, painted warriors. David carried, pulled, and lent a shoulder to several badly cut men as he escorted them to the rear. He broke open bandages in furious haste as he put heavy pressure on sliced arms, legs, and abdomens. The noise of the battle only a few feet from his tent went practically unnoticed as he worked on the men. Some of the wounded whose bandages could be tied tightly ran back to resume their places in the line. By dawn, the fighting was over, with Wayne in a strong position facing a British detachment sent up to reinforce the Indians. Instead of counting his losses, Wayne ordered the British lines charged. The impetuous charge of men supposedly mauled by a night attack so surprised the British that they hastily withdrew into the safer confines of the town.

On July 11, 1782, the British evacuated their troops by sea, and soon afterwards, the Pennsylvanians victoriously entered the city. David preached in several Baptist churches in the area during the following weeks, and he ministered often to General Wayne, who was stricken with a malarial fever. Though David's thin frame could not gain weight, his complexion was pale, and an occasional fever and coughing engulfed him, he was fit for duty more often than most of those around him. A strong physical and mental constitution lay deep within this chaplain-doctor who had grown to love the marches, the fighting, and the camaraderie of men laying their lives on the line for a cause in which they believed. Perhaps it was not that he was healthy, for he was not, but rather that he was engaged in something he believed in with all his faculties, that made him continue to function when lesser men would have sought a bed, a furlough, or a discharge.

With Georgia secured for the Americans, David's unit was ordered to join Greene once again in Charlestown. David rode beside his feverish commander on the march northward, mixing quinine and warm rum to fight the lingering malaria. They arrived in Charlestown on December 14, and David was immediately reassigned to the Third Pennsylvania Regiment stationed at Fort Pitt in western Pennsylvania. His time en route to Fort Pitt allowed him a week at home to visit with his family, church, and friends. He was surprised at the civilian celebrations that continued over the victories of the American armies at Yorktown and in the south. Being a part of a moving, fighting army, David had no time, and little inclination, to be concerned about the magnitude of the conquests of which he had been a part. He enjoyed serving as a reporter, however, for the recent events in the south, and his appearance was sought almost daily in a church or community meetinghouse to speak while he was home.

He arrived at Fort Pitt in mid-January, serving as the regimental chaplain for Colonel Richard Butler's troops. Preaching to the troops, reporting on his unit's activities in Georgia, and assisting with the sick in the medical detachment kept David busy until June. Most of the soldiers, including David, were given a six-month furlough in the summer, anticipating a discharge by the end of the year. The Fourth of July celebration in Tredyffryn, Chester County, had as its chaplain for the day, the Reverend Doctor David Jones, home from the war at last.

6

Indian Wars

The first priority of the Jones family after the war was to move to a new house and farm in Easttown, Chester County. While on leave from the Army in 1781, and at the suggestion of General Wayne, David traded his property in the Great Valley for a large parcel of land on Leopard Road near Wayne's home. Moving his family was delayed until after the war. But now that David was home, he began enlarging the small house on his new property as well as building a large barn to accommodate his animals, equipment, and feed. Since David had been away so long in the army, his one-year tenure as pastor at Great Valley had ended. He was still not anxious to settle into a permanent pastorship just yet, with the new farm commanding his attention. Therefore, the church called Nicholas Cox to be its minister for one year, beginning in May, 1783. Cox's disagreement with the Welshmen over doctrinal matters, however, soon ended his stay with them. David and others frequently preached for the church during the dispute. David was content to build his farm and supply the pulpits of many churches in the area for the next two years.

Several Welsh Baptist friends visited David in the spring of 1786, telling of the great need for experienced Baptist pastors in several pastorless churches. One church sent a delegation to visit him in March to request that he consider becoming their settled pastor. Though David did not encourage them, they returned in two weeks inviting him to fill their pulpit at Southampton, Pennsylvania, as a supply preacher. David's desire to preach, coupled with Ann's longing to settle in one place during the young adult years of the two older girls, impressed the family that they should heed the church's call. It was not difficult to find a good family to rent their farm at Easttown, and so they arrived on April 9, 1786, at their new pastoral charge.

Southampton Baptist Church, twenty-five miles northeast of

Great Valley, enjoyed a distinguished history among early American Baptists before David's arrival. Though small in size, it had established an early Latin grammar school for the community, and several notable pastors grew up in that congregation, including David's former teacher, Isaac Eaton. Samuel Jones, David's ex-schoolmate at Hopewell had served as the pastor from 1763 to 1770. The new yellow meetinghouse, erected in 1773, was the source of a special pride to the church. A rock wall separated the church and a small cemetery from a large, two-story parsonage built of native rock. The Jones family was given free usage of the parsonage and profits of the farm along with a salary of forty sterling pounds per year. With the additional rent from their own farm in Chester County, a degree of prosperity was attained after eight difficult war years.

Farming and preaching occupied David's time following the war, but Ann noticed a trait in him that had not changed during those years of separation. In fact, his desire to travel had been heightened during his movement over the length and breadth of the young nation with his military units. His anxious wife noted with growing concern that a settled pastorate might be impossible for one so accustomed to constant tours for God and country. Since his first missionary effort to the Ohio country in 1772, he had desired to own property in the West. George Rogers Clark surveyed a plot on Licking Creek not far

Southampton Baptist Church

from the Muskingum River, and now that David had a small savings, he talked of going to file on that land.

"Go now, David? Leave here when you haven't been with the church for even a month? That's nonsense," Ann said.

"Oh, it's not nonsensical, Ann. I told the elders when we came that I might need some time off on this property transaction."

"I suppose you're going to tell them that you have a ministry to the Indians, too?"

"Well, I don't like your sarcasm, and I probably will preach to them, you know."

Ann was angry. She remained silent.

"There is a deacons' meeting Sunday afternoon, and if they give me their approval as they said they would, I think I'll go." He paused. "You did agree with me that it would be a good investment, didn't you?"

She didn't answer. Rising from her chair in the parlor, she walked into the kitchen, shaking her head in frustration. David spread out the large map of the Ohio River on the table and studied it carefully.

The deacons were not anxious for their new pastor to be gone, but they were very grateful to have him, and some of them had given their promise earlier that he could go. Then, too, David had this one redeeming feature of his ministry: he could preach with effectiveness. Though he was often absent from his pulpit, when he did preach, his thorough study, flashing eyes, and piercing voice earned unusual praise from members and visitors. Not many ever slept under his preaching, for he was endowed with a rare gift of communicating his mind and feelings to others. He was easy to know, with a sharp mind and commanding personality. In addition to his excellent performance in the pulpit and community, his reputation as a "fighting parson" who had been faithful through the entire revolution enhanced his chances for the deacons to allow his frequent leaves of absence.

The trip to the West was brief, as David visited friends at Fort Pitt and several farmers and hunters along the route, purchased his land, and was back by June 15. His accounts of preaching in private homes, Indian camps, and rural churches made his members feel they had played an important role in his ministry by sending him. His reputation among Baptists continued to grow as invitations to preach mounted. Individuals, interested in entertaining neighbors, often invited David to preach at the conclusion of a Saturday afternoon tea. His accounts of the war and western Indians, combined with a forthright presentation of the gospel, often accounted for the presence of some of the partygoers in church the next morning. As a result of such speaking engagements, David preached more sermons away from Southampton than he did at his home church from the middle of June to the beginning of 1787.

His desire for an active life and the need for some semblance of stability found a satisfying balance at Southampton. He remarked to Ann one winter evening that as much as he enjoyed preaching and traveling, there was no adequate comparison between the comforts of home and the misery of a dirty, smoking, frozen hut in the army's winter quarters. The analogy didn't particularly please Ann, but she was content to have her husband by the fire that night. By spring, David was already determined to make an annual affair of his trip to the West. He left in May, preaching at least once each day in homes and churches along his route to Fort Pitt and down the Ohio to his Licking Creek property.

As the months passed at Southampton, David maintained his frenetic pace of preaching, farming, traveling, and ministering to the needs of his pastoral charge. Many were surprised that the same man whose eyes flashed in the pulpit could be a great comfort in time of trial. Possessing a warm bedside manner with the sick, David did not practice medicine except in cases of emergency, but many a patient was calmed following a quiet reading of Scripture and prayer by Reverend Jones. Ann treasured those undisturbed moments by his side, knowing that he would soon be off again to thunder forth the gospel in his inimitable positive fashion.

The trips to Ohio began to get longer each year as westerners began to plan for his visits there. In 1790, he toured the northern areas of Kentucky at the request of several Pennsylvania families who had moved to the new area, now clamoring for statehood. Whether it was his prolonged absences, minor doctrinal differences, or a combination of many factors, David was not sure, but his ministry at Southampton was obviously coming to an end. In 1792, he stood by a fellow member when excommunication proceedings were begun, and the enmity of those prosecuting his friend, Peter Sauerman, proved to be uncomfortable. His strong Calvinistic doctrine was a bit too powerful for several members, and when his tenants in Chester County wrote that they would be moving from his farm in April, 1792, the family decided that he should resign his church and return to Easttown. No permanent enmities were involved, however, as evidenced by his frequent return to preach for the Southampton church in subsequent years.

The Baptist Church in the Great Valley had continued services with the aid of transient ministers during the years of David's ministry in Southampton. David, as well as others, often rode the twenty-five miles on Sunday to preach for them during those years. No sooner had the Jones family arrived there than the Great Valley church asked David to become their settled pastor. David hesitated to accept their offer for several months, finally agreeing in July, 1793, the church recognizing "the limitations of the roughness of the roads and the distance from his house to the church, he will serve us until a more favorable situation presents itself." Both parties continued with a "more favorable situation" for the next twenty-eight years.

Before settling into his new role at Great Valley, David had yet another trip to take. This time he fulfilled an invitation of Virginia Baptists to take a speaking tour through their Piedmont and mountain sections. Of course, he also planned to go on to Kentucky and Ohio before returning home, especially since he had a lawsuit over his property boundaries in Ohio. A nostalgic day preaching at the new meetinghouse at Brandywine Creek was his first stop before continuing on to Alexandria, Richmond, Virginia's back country, Wheeling, and Fort Pitt. He easily won his legal suit in September with the defendant paying all the court costs. He was gone until October, and then he hurried home for a very important date—the wedding of his firstborn, Eleanor, on November 21, 1793.

Eleanor was thirty-one years old in December, 1792, a young woman beginning to accept the possibility of remaining forever unmarried. She had known young John Garrett of Delaware for many years through family relationships in the Welsh Tract. When he served with the Continental army at Valley Forge in the winter of 1777–1778, he occasionally came home with David for supplies. Displaying a growing interest in Eleanor, he visited her several times in the Great Valley before her family departed for Southampton. Their engagement was announced in Southampton, and since Garrett was living near the Great Valley in 1792, Eleanor encouraged her father in the move back to their family farm.

The Jones farm was bordered on the west and north by the Leopard and Haverford roads, and it was there, rather than at the church, that the wedding was to be celebrated. That place was the scene of much busy and happy activity for many weeks prior to November 21 as a wedding dress, new furniture, polished pewter, tablecloths, and new paint formed only a portion of the list of "things to do." David had contributed at least two things to the wedding preparations: he was safely out of the women's way on his preaching tour, this time with Ann's blessings, and he left sufficient funds with Ann and Eleanor for a healthy nuptial budget. With David away, Ann and Eleanor attacked their objective with an almost childlike enthusiasm.

An extension dining table that enlarged from four to eight feet was purchased and hauled from Philadelphia. The big front door was painted a light green and further adorned with a bright, round brass handle. Six new armchairs with cane seats were delivered just before the wedding. Nineteen-year-old David and sixteen-year-old Horatio were entrusted with the responsibility of polishing the pewter. Gathering horsetail rushes from nearby creek banks, they rubbed their mother's old pewter dishes, serving bowls, and utensils until they passed Ann's careful inspection. A new eight-place garnish completed the needed dishes for all the expected guests. The usual coarse cotton tablecloth gave way to two white damask fabrics trimmed with lace. Special scented candles were carefully poured in the smokehouse and mounted in brass and pewter holders as the day drew near.

On the wedding day, Ann smoothed the last wrinkle out of Eleanor's dress as she stepped back to take a final survey of the lovely bride. The white satin dress hung straight to the floor in front. Trimmed with lace edging around the curved low neck and long sleeves, a bustle and short train completed the bride's gown. Eleanor's hair was puffed and rolled in back, and a tiny cotton cap held a flowing white veil. Her friend, Jane, was dressed in orange velvet with white lace trimming. Ann smiled as she surveyed the labor of many months of hard work. Her daughter's loveliness was deep within her, for while she was not truly a pretty young woman, her personality and loving nature made her one of the finest young ladies of the area.

"Eleanor, you are beautiful, and I think everything's ready. Before I go, though, I have something to say. I'm proud of the way all these lovely trappings have turned out. We've worked hard, haven't we?"

They exchanged knowing smiles.

"But, Eleanor, I am prouder of another beauty about you. Your real God-given grace is deep within you. I don't know that your father and I can take credit for it, but your sweetness, gentleness, and love have been some of our greatest prides. You've been especially good to me, and for me, and I want you to know that I love you more than I can say. You've been my closest friend for these years, and, well, I just thank God that you are my daughter."

She kissed her quickly on the cheek and stepped out into the crowded parlor, touching her eyes with her handkerchief. Sitting in her appointed place, she noted with pride her husband and son-in-law. David was dressed in a tweed black and white coat with a plain white cravat. His knee-length britches were black, accentuating the white silk stockings and silver buckles on his black shoes. John wore a dark blue double-breasted coat that fell back at the hips. His shirt had large white ruffles at the collar and sleeves. He was shorter and stockier than David. The two men had become close friends, and had just been talking of riding together to Kentucky one day soon. David held his favorite Welsh Bible as he prepared to conduct the service of the marriage of his beloved Eleanor to his friend, John Garrett.

The service and fellowship that followed pleased family and friends alike. The women served thick stew and apple and peach pies until the couple bid their farewells at last and drove off into the gathering darkness. When all the guests had departed, the tables had been cleaned, and the food put away, David put his arms around Ann and looked into her eyes.

"It went well, didn't it, Annie?" he said.

"Oh, I hope so. I do hope so."

"Isn't this the time to thank me for what I did to help all this wedding preparation?"

He grinned as she pulled away, not sure whether he was serious or not.

"*YOU* did! What in the world did *YOU* do?"

"Well, I went to Ohio, of course."

Both of them laughed as David embraced her again.

"You didn't do too badly, yourself, Anniefach. By the way, to me you're still the prettiest woman at any wedding."

Ann was most pleased at one of David's rare moments of humor. It made the perfect conclusion to a wonderful day for her.

Throughout 1793, the new United States of America was struggling for survival against huge odds. Opposing political factions led by Thomas Jefferson and Alexander Hamilton were threatening to explode any hope of a sound fiscal policy, and the British, with their powerful navy, were violating neutral rights of American shipping on the high seas. While French and English factions vied for control of the infant country's favor, Pennsylvanians were concerned with a more serious threat to the West. American frontiersmen poured into the areas beyond the Ohio River in increasing and alarming numbers. Eleanor and John Garrett later joined that flow of settlers to Ohio, upsetting the Indians who began retaliating to guarantee the security of their land. Great Britain also refused to give up her northwestern military posts in violation of the Peace of Paris which ended the Revolutionary War.

Anti-English sentiment spread as news that the British commanders were supplying wampum belts, blankets, muskets, and vermilion war paint from government arsenals to the enemies of a country with which His Britannic Majesty was, supposedly, at peace. General Josiah Harmar's expedition against the Indians did little to stop the bloodshed in 1790, and when General Arthur St. Clair suffered a military disaster along the Maumee River of Ohio in 1791 with a loss of six hundred men, alarm spread among the inhabitants of western Pennsylvania. General "Mad Anthony" Wayne was appointed army commander to raise troops and to put an end to the western warfare. He asked for his friend and neighbor, David Jones, to serve as the army's chaplain in the place of John Hurt, recently resigned. When David accepted, he became the second chaplain of the United States Army, organized after the Constitution in 1790.

Wayne established winter quarters north of Cincinnati in the fall of 1793 while David was involved with Eleanor's wedding. David debated the offer of the chaplaincy for several months, but as spring approached, he received the church's permission to join the army in Ohio. One of the factors involved in his decision concerned the role of Baptists in the new nation. Having been a small minority in colonial America, Baptists had strongly extended their influence since the "Great Awakening" in the 1740s. In many parts of Europe, Baptists continued to suffer some active persecution and much condemnation as dissenters. Prior to his departure on June 18, 1794, David wrote to a leading Baptist minister, Dr. John Riggson, expressing something of that sentiment as well as other reasons for his rejoining the army.

"Dr. Riggson: I am now appointed chaplain to the army and am the only one in America. By this you may learn that our society appears in a different point of view than yours in England, where you are bound with the odious character of a dissenter.... I am also going to the West for the following reasons: (1) My health is improved and traveling in times past has had a good effect on it. (2) The army lies opposite Kentucky where I have business to transact. (3) I am a neighbor to the Commander-in-Chief, General Wayne, whose chaplain I was during the last war, and to whom I am much attached, and (4) I am in hopes once more of having an opportunity to speak to the Indians, should I live to the end of the war."

One last thing remained, however, prior to his departure—saying good-bye to an unhappy Ann. The tension hung heavily in the hot room as David appeared at the door of the kitchen where Ann was standing by the oven. She appeared to be working, but in reality was only pretending to be busily engaged while fighting back tears of frustration and disappointment.

"Ann, I'm ready to go now," he said.

Tears began streaming down her cheeks.

"Why, David, why?" she asked softly.

"We've been through all that before now, haven't we?"

"Yes," she answered, "for thirty-two years we've been through all this. David, you're fifty-eight years old, and you've been gone for long trips that get longer with each passing year. You've gone to fight the British; you've gone to clear land in the Ohio country; you've preached all over the country; you've gone to preach to the Indians; and now you're going to fight them. David, you have been gone for most of fifteen of our thirty-two years of marriage. Why, David? Other ministers aren't gone that much. Why do you have to get involved in everything?"

"Ann, turn around and look at me." His voice was firm and commanding. She turned, wiping her tears on the long apron clutched in her hands, but she did not look him directly in the eyes.

"Ann, you know very well that I was called to preach the Word of God, and in every absence I was preaching. Even on those trips to Ohio, I preached more than seven times each week. You knew you were marrying a minister when we wed. Now why must you make this unpleasant just as I leave?"

"I thought when we married that you would be more interested in pastoring farmers than campaigning with soldiers."

His response was sharp, "I am interested in preaching God's Word wherever it takes me."

She whirled around in exasperation and faced the stove, busying herself with the pans nearby. Now she raised her voice and said sarcastically, "Yes, David, you go preach God's Word to the soldiers in the West, and I'll get the ploughing done, feed the livestock, pay the bills, and try to keep this whole farm together."

"Ann, do you realize that I, a *BAPTIST*, have been invited by General Wayne to be the only chaplain in the entire army? Baptists are being recognized more and more, and I'm part of that—we're all a part of that. You know that I've arranged for Horatio to take care of the heavy chores, and I'll likely be back in the winter. He's strong and he knows what to do. Besides, I have enlisted. You have to accept that. The fact is that I am committed to go."

"Then go," she said in a whisper.

David pulled his tall, thin frame erect. He looked outside, where Horatio stood by his horse, and then glanced at Ann, still turned away from him. He gently placed the small bag on the floor and silently strode over to his wife. He enveloped her in his long arms.

Traveling on horseback, he arrived at camp after preaching at almost every stop along the way. He was both gratified to hear of a significant army victory over the Indians at Fallen Timbers and disappointed that he had not arrived in time to participate in the engagement. An uneasy calm settled over the troops as scattered bands of Indians continued to roam the immediate vicinity. A letter arrived from home bearing the unhappy news that Ann's oldest sister had died, as had a niece of David's in Delaware. News of young David's continued poor health indicated that his eyes were now failing, necessitating the curtailment of his study with Dr. David Davis. Ann was fearful that he was in danger of losing his eyesight altogether. David wrote in his diary, "God, in your mercy, grant me that the tribulations of this life may work together for good to me."

In Pennsylvania, Ann was moving through her daily routine with a growing sense of uneasiness over David's welfare, young David's health, the productivity of the farm, and a growing feeling of loneliness. Several friends and neighbors attempted to fill her Sundays with chatty visits after worship services, but one visit was far more significant than the others. Seth Adamson rode from near the Paoli Tavern down Leopard Road, turned right, and rode by the Joneses' barn. Ann looked up in surprise, puzzled that Deacon Adamson would appear in the middle of the day. She walked out on the back porch to greet him.

"Hello, Horatio. Good day to you, Sister Jones. Horatio, do you think your mum might have a cup of tea around here somewhere?"

Ann tensed with fear that Seth might be the bearer of bad news concerning David, and hence her usual quick invitation to "Come on in!" was slow in coming. She spoke seriously, "Seth, do you have some news about David?"

"Nope. Haven't heard a thing," he replied and paused a moment. "Oh, Ann, I didn't think about your worry over David. I'm sorry I caused you one moment's worry. No, Ann, I'm not here about David's safety. I'm sure if he could fight clean through the Revolution, he and Wayne will handle those Indians OK."

Ann's countenance brightened, relieved that David was all right so far as she knew. "Come on in, Seth," she invited, "there's always tea for you."

Seated around the kitchen table in a very informal chat with Ann and Horatio, Deacon Adamson spoke to Ann at last in a serious tone, "Well, Ann, this is a delightful conversation, but there is something specific I came to say."

Horatio spoke up quickly. "Should I be excused, Mum?"

"No, no, please stay, Horatio. I want you to hear this, too." He paused. "Ann, you might want to tell me that what I'm about to say is none of my business, but I'd like to offer you some advice. It's not that you haven't thought it all through many times before, but I'd like to say it anyway."

"What is it, Seth? Of course I'll take advice from you. You and Pauline have been dear friends for years and years."

"Well, it's like this. I'll be honest with you. I've heard through Pauline that you have been very upset over David's going back into the army. The word I have is that his being gone so much has been a festering sore spot with you for years. That right, Ann? Please tell me straight."

"Well, it has been a problem with the children, too, and with the farm, this sickness. . . ."

"Yes, I know his being away has been a special problem to you, of all people, though. But there are some things that you ought to hear. Now you know, Ann, that I know David very well. I know he's quick-tempered and restless. He's talented; he's smart; and he's a hard worker. I also know that God gave that man a special itch to jump on his horse every time an Indian or an Englishman shoots a gun or an arrow and go be a chaplain to somebody."

Ann and Horatio exchanged smiling glances and nodded.

"But here's the point, Ann and Horatio. You know it takes somebody with boundless energy and talent in every generation and in every place to get things done. No church, no government, no state ever progressed unless somebody was willing to give something extra of their time and talent. Their families have suffered, and will always have to suffer their being gone more than the average person. Of course, that's just it; those men aren't average, they're special. Nobody asks me or the other Baptist deacons and neighbors to be the only chaplain in the United States Army, or the only anything. But David's a special Baptist leader, Ann.

"Now you take Dr. Manning in Rhode Island. Do you suppose his wife had him at home every night when he was trying to build that college? No, I'm sure he was gone about as much as David, and now because of his hard work, we've got a Baptist college for young ministers. Still, Mrs. Manning and the young Mannings had to do without their husband and Pa for all of us to be blessed with that college.

"Many of those churches that David has gone to preach to are one day going to be strong churches, Ann, because of men like him who rode a horse through bad weather and war and kept them going. One day some missionary to the Indians will be sent out by the Philadelphia Association, and he will thank David for breaking the trail back in '72 and '73. A lot of soldiers probably know God today because of David's sermons when all they had otherwise were camp followers and liquor. Right now he may be bandaging up somebody with one hand and reading the Bible to them out of the other. Come to think of it, some of them might get more pain out of God's Word than an Indian's tomahawk."

They all laughed. Mr. Adamson paused for a moment.

"You know, David has played, and is playing, a part like the light infantry in the war. They run out in front, sort of disorganized-like and soften up the enemy's lines. They're crack shots, but they don't have bayonets on their rifles; so they frequently get killed by bayonet charges from the enemy. But when they get the enemy all upset, then the regulars come marching up in those pretty ranks and punch right through. Then everybody applauds the regulars and the generals, but it seems like nobody notices all those dead and wounded light infantry. But they made it all possible. David sort of reminds me of them. He's jumped around from farming to doctoring, from chaplain to settled pastor, to traveling evangelist and all that, but he sure is going to make it a whole lot easier for the people that follow."

He paused again for several seconds to let his two-person audience reflect on his thoughts. The silence assured him that he was making an impression as he continued.

"Ann, I feel sympathy for your loneliness. You've put up with a lot of hard times all by yourself, and I admire you. Just know this; you've got a big stake in all that David does. You may not get the credit that he does, but you've made David what he is. You've given him love, strength, stability. Well, the Jones family is something special to us here and to the Baptist cause everywhere in this country. I'm proud of you both; of David for how he's gone out and given himself, and for you and the children for keeping the home steady and happy. One of these days, people will appreciate what you've all done. I'm proud that you're my pastor's family."

He looked up to see Ann's eyes misty. Horatio had his head bowed. They thanked Deacon Adamson for coming, grateful for his words of encouragement. When he rode off, Ann remained inside, facing westward with tears streaming down her face, and she spoke softly, "Oh, David. Oh, David. I love you, dear David. Please do your best for us all, and come home to us. I love you; I'm proud of you, my David."

David was, indeed, preaching to Indians and ministering to physically and spiritually ill soldiers. He was confined to the immediate vicinity of the fort at Greenville due to the roving Indian bands in the aftermath of the Battle of Fallen Timbers. He did his job to the satisfaction of most, but in November a complaint was brought against the chaplain by a woman in Greenville. Alleging that as he passed through her settlement earlier he had refused to baptize her children, she complained to Major Josiah Bewell. The major used the occasion of an evening meal with David, General Wayne, and Major John Hugh to make the charges known. Methodist Bewell was offended with the Baptist minister's refusal to conduct rites for all religious persuasions in their various ritual forms.

Bewell spoke in a tone designed to give intellectual battle on the issue, "An army chaplain isn't a Baptist, Methodist, or Catholic. He is a chaplain who agrees to minister to all religious beliefs."

"Well, Major, your argument is wrong for more than one reason," replied David. "First, my pledge as a chaplain concerns soldiers, not civilians, and so your complaint reflects a personal dislike for my actions rather than my legal responsibilities, doesn't it?"

General Wayne and the other officers leaned back in their chairs with pleasant expressions, anticipating an interesting repartee between two theological combatants.

"No, it does not."

"Oh, I think it does, but let me continue to defend my actions. It will be quite simple. My allegiance to the United States of America, the army, and my commander is superceded by my allegiance to Jesus Christ. No one, I repeat, no one, has a right to add to or detract from His orders as an individual conscience interprets them. I interpret the baptismal order in Scripture as immersion of consenting believers, and therefore I will not practice some other form of baptism which I believe, by conscience, to be in error. You as a Methodist, through interpretation, or ignorance, sprinkle a little water on babies' heads, and I wouldn't expect you to immerse one of my parishioners. In fact, not being accustomed to but a mere cup of water, you could be dangerous in a pool."

"I fail to see the levity in such a serious charge, Chaplain. My ability to slosh somebody in a creek isn't in question here. Your actions are. Are you wiser than all other generations and chaplains who have baptized children?"

"I am a servant to the truth as I understand it in Christ and his Word. When I am convinced that either of those authorities teach sprinkling, I will practice it. Until then, my conscience will be followed."

"It is one duty of a chaplain to baptize anyone when requested."

"Which duty? Based on the Bible, your ideas, or on some other Methodist? To which are you referring? To which shall I give allegiance? To the President of the United States or God? To General Wayne or Christ?"

"A court-martial might help you find your proper allegiance."

General Wayne leaned forward, pouring wine in each man's glass, and said, "Gentlemen, I perceive that we cannot settle this matter amicably here since my authority in the matter seems to have been supplanted by a higher officer." There was a twinkle in his eye as he pointed skyward. He lifted his glass. "Here is to peace with the Shawnees, Ottawas, and Miamis."

David spent the next few weeks reading several of the Greek classical biographies: Plutarch, Cato, Demosthenes, and Mark Anthony. He also attended to his chaplain's duties of performing wedding ceremonies for the soldiers, preaching, officiating at burials, and counseling white captives coming into camp almost every week since the Battle of Fallen Timbers. In November, he served in the capacity he disliked most—chaplain at an execution.

Sergeant Keating was the brother of a friend of David's, a Catholic priest in Philadelphia. The sergeant had served well in the Revolutionary War but had become an alcoholic. Strong drink caused him to be convicted of mutiny and cow stealing. Corporal Reading, recognized earlier as a brave soldier, was a nineteen-year-old convicted of leaving his post and stealing and killing a cow belonging to a Mr. Tharp. Sergeant Keating was sentenced to be shot, while Reading was to be hanged. Keating, especially, was extremely sorrowful, spending much time on his knees in prayer with Chaplain Jones prior to the appointed day. Appeals were made on behalf of both men, but no one expected "Mad Anthony" to change his mind.

Sunday, November 30, was a cold, rainy day as the grim procession began its march to the gallows, a half-mile distant. Sergeant Keating was kept waiting out of sight until after Reading's hanging. At the scaffold, David preached a twenty-minute sermon and prayed as earnestly as he could. Reading was ordered to mount the wagon, the warrant was read, and the hood and rope were placed around his head and neck. There was a pause. General "Mad Anthony" Wayne stepped to the wagon and read a full and complete pardon. Many of the men assembled as witnesses wept openly with relief. David, too, felt a sense of joy he had seldom experienced as they untied Reading and ushered him to his unit.

Then Sergeant Keating was ordered to march up to the execution spot. David's outward prayer was one of God's forgiveness, and his inward desire was for General Wayne to possess one more pardon. Keating was ordered to his knees, a cap drawn over his face. Wayne made no move. *Why?* David thought. *Why not Keating as well as Reading? Is it that he is older? Is that it?*

"Ready . . . Aim . . ."

"Halt!" said Wayne. He stepped between the firing squad and Keating and read the pardon. The general left without further word. Overwhelming joy greeted the scene as old comrades-in-arms rushed to greet the emotionally exhausted sergeant. David was rendered immobile as he felt that his feet had grown roots in the soggy soil and his knees and legs had gone limp. "Thank you, God," he muttered. He vowed that he would forever change the appellation "Mad Anthony" to "Forgiving Anthony."

The winter months found the army encamped, waiting for the Indian tribes to respond to Wayne's invitation for a treaty parley. David continued his work on the Shawnee language begun on his missionary endeavor in 1772. Several of the tribes began coming in by early summer of 1795. In July, the conference began at Greenville. David noted in his diary that land thought by whites to be clearly defined by the Indians was in hot dispute among the Ottawa, Chippewa, and Shawnee tribes. General Wayne was hard pressed to keep peace within the various quarreling groups.

On August 3, however, a significant treaty was signed by all parties. By this Treaty of Greenville, the Indians ceded the southeastern corner of the Northwest Territory, together with sixteen enclaves, such as Vincennes, Detroit, and the site of Chicago, in return for annuities totaling ten thousand dollars. David was proud to be a part of the successful effort to bring victory from the previous defeats of the army at the hands of the Indians. Twenty years of fighting along the Muskingum, Scioto, and Ohio rivers were at an end, and David had been a part of the success. He felt a renewed kinship and camaraderie with his army associates, and an ever greater pride in his new country. Little did he realize that the swarms of new settlers up the Ohio River valleys would, in ten years, make the Treaty of Greenville a mere scrap of paper because of their insatiable greed.

Two days after the signing of the treaty, celebrations of the peace were held in abeyance as the wife of Little Turtle, the Miami Chief, died suddenly. General Wayne ordered the army to accompany the Indian mourners to the grave with military music. Three cannons were fired in her honor. On returning from the grave site, David preached a sermon concerning the meaning of death and the hope of a new life in Christ, who overcame death. At the conclusion of David's sermon and prayer, Little Turtle arose and approached David. Clasping David firmly in a gesture of thanks, the interpreter relayed the chief's profuse words of gratitude for the message.

A continued ministry to the recently released captives ensued during the autumn, and with each returnee, David's hatred of the British mounted. Betsy Heartt was one of those returned, and David described her ordeal at length in his diary. Her husband and five children were killed by the Indians, who gave her no meat or bread during her five years of captivity. She lived on acorns, nuts, and what she could steal at night from the "leftover pigeon and raccoon guts." The shroud they gave her would not cover half her body as she was constantly forced to hard labor. David concluded Betsy's story by saying, "These are the Quaker saints, of whom the Philadelphians speak. May God remember all their deeds! And may He reward a double portion to the Savage Kingdom of Great Britain!"

The winter of 1795–1796 was a mild one in the Ohio River Valley as David took a brief leave to visit Baptist churches in Kentucky and to purchase additional land on Grave Creek near Wheeling. In the spring, he ministered to his commander in both physical and spiritual needs as Wayne suffered with a severe bronchial ailment. He also detected a note of cool reserve on the part of the general toward him. When Wayne's condition improved, David was sent on an errand through the wilderness to Detroit, where he wrote to his friend and commander expressing concern over the apparent tension between them. He received a letter in reply requesting David to return to the camp and "clear up the matter."

Many months prior to the Treaty of Greenville, a Robert Newman was apprehended by the American army, and it was soon discovered that he was a deserter who had joined the British and Indians during St. Clair's campaign. A Mr. Harrison took a deposition from the captured Newman at the falls of the Ohio stating that Generals Wayne and Wilkinson had ordered him to defect to the enemy in order to spy for the Americans. Harrison shared that information with David, who immediately reported the contents of the message to General Wilkinson, the nearest commander to David at the time. He did not, however, report it to Wayne on his return to his own unit. When Wayne was later questioned about his part in "the Newman affair as recounted by your chaplain," he was understandably upset.

General Wayne invited David to dine with him and discuss the entire situation. David explained at length where he heard the information and his actions in reporting it to the nearest headquarters. Wayne asked David to draw up a certificate stating the facts. After several corrections, the general was satisfied that the government would recognize that Newman's story was merely fabricated to save himself from the charges of treason and desertion. The old friendship between chaplain and general was renewed over a cup of hot tea and pleasant conversation. David was happy to leave for home with those old ties firmly entrenched, for not long after he arrived in Pennsylvania, news came that Wayne was dead on the shores of Lake Erie, the victim of pneumonia.

7

The Old War Horse

A civilian once again, David entered into the life of a settled pastor more comfortably than ever before. He was older, sixty-one years old in 1797, but his decrease in energy was only slight, as he was off to Ohio for a brief visit to his new property in September. The church, still pleased to have David as its pastor, secured the services of Reverend John Boggs to assist them in David's absences. When David was there, he visited inactive church members, administered the ordinances, and preached often and well.

The Philadelphia Baptist Association met at New Mills, Burlington County, New Jersey, in 1798, electing David as its new moderator. By the nature of Baptist polity, each local church is completely independent of all outside authority, and even though the offices of the association, therefore, had no particular authority, it was a signal honor to be selected as the leader of the annual meeting. As spokesman for the largest Baptist association in the country, David preached the annual sermon on the subject of the sabbath day. Citing biblical precedents for worshiping on the first day of the week, he received the approbation of the assembled messengers from the many churches represented for his doctrinal thoughts. He left immediately following the meeting to represent his association in Augusta County, Virginia, at its annual Baptist meeting. It took very little encouragement for Reverend Jones to mount up with a Bible and ride off to preach in some distant pulpit.

The aging process was beginning to tell on David and Ann. David was still tall, very thin, and nagged with his wheezing cough, while Ann retained good health. She was heavier now, but still a hardworking, calm, and good-natured wife, mother, and friend. While he was working on his large barn in the autumn of 1799, a rusty, brass doorplating slipped, cutting the middle finger of his left hand. Infection set in with swelling, and at last, a bad fever. He was confined to the farm for several weeks with a wound that should have healed earlier. The following winter, Ann was standing at the kitchen stove on an early Sunday morning preparing biscuits in the small oven when she felt her left arm go numb; then her left leg lost all feeling. She tried to turn to call David for help, but no sound came from her moving lips. She eased herself to the floor. The odor of burning bread reached David in the bedroom as he read over his sermon notes.

"Ann, what's burning?" he called. There was no response.

"David! Horatio! Go see what's burning. See if your mum needs help."

Still no response. He set his papers aside and strode quickly into the kitchen. Ann was lying on the floor beside a smoking stove. Her mouth was moving without a sound; her eyes were wide and frightened. She had vomited.

"Annie! Oh, Annie!" David rushed to her side. The two boys arrived as David picked up her limp form and almost ran to the bedroom.

"Tend the kitchen, Horatio!" he called as he moved. "David, get some towels and water!"

He rubbed her limp arm and leg with hot towels and rubbing oil for several minutes, and soon she was able to speak as the numbness dissipated. David held her tightly as she wept in relief over her recovery from the horrifying experience. Before an hour had passed, she walked carefully around the room, testing her strength. Her husband and the boys, relieved that she was feeling better, moved back to the kitchen, where Ann insisted that she help clean up the ruins of breakfast. Though David firmly protested, she began scraping off the dishes on the table as the men worked on the stove and counter.

"David!" Her pitiful cry struck terror into the three men.

They turned to see her crumple to the floor. Though she would live for another nine years, she would be a semi-invalid, a victim of a paralytic stroke.

The family was on solid financial ground, thankfully, by 1800, since their farm income, small salary at the church, and rental of their farms in Ohio and western Pennsylvania brought in more than enough money to meet their needs. Thus, with economic stability, and with Ann's sickness and the war ended for the moment, David sought new foes to fight and conquer. He had an innate need for enemies, and a good opponent always whetted him and brought out his best talents. The anger involved in a good fight was a strength and healing for the restless parson. With the British quiet for a time, he turned from military to theological adversaries.

Many Christians of David's day interpreted the ministry of the Holy Spirit of God as a second blessing that brought extraordinary gifts to the believer. He preached many sermons on the subject, emphasizing that the Holy Spirit had, as his most prominent ministry, the role of comforter, not the giver of special blessings. Special gifts such as healings, speaking in tongues, and prophecy of the future, David believed, were first-century phenomena needed to confirm the entire Christ-Holy Spirit events recorded in the Bible. For those views, he had been condemned by many in the Philadelphia area as a "legalistic preacher of the Gospel without fire and emotion."

With the encouragement of his son, Horatio, who was ordained as a minister by the Great Valley Church in 1800, and others, David sat at his small, round table in the parlor and wrote his first book on the subject of the Holy Spirit. The publication was greeted by praise from his friends and silence by those opposing his views. Though he was engaged in building a new meetinghouse at Great Valley to replace the log building constructed in 1722, he launched yet another book.

David's boyhood friend, Samuel Jones, wrote a pamphlet decrying the Welsh Baptist practice of the ordinance of laying on of hands. Samuel's Welsh heritage did not prevent his pointing out that the issue was a divisive force in the Philadelphia Association, with half of the churches abstaining from the practice. David was incensed over what he considered the perfidious stand of a Welshman. Not only was Samuel theologically incorrect, David felt, but also his disloyalty to his heritage should not go unchallenged. The fact that Samuel was a friend, the recipient of an honorary doctorate from Rhode Island College, and a well-known and respected Baptist pastor did not deter David from attacking him in print as if he were a British general advocating the invasion of Chester County. Besides, Rhode Island College had just conferred an honorary degree of Master of Arts on David, and perhaps he was feeling competent to enter the world of fighting men of letters.

Welsh Baptists believed that laying on of hands by believers as a symbol of sanction and sanctification should follow profession of faith and baptism by immersion before one could become a member in good standing of a Baptist church. David employed the vehicle of sarcasm in his book in defense of "Hands," a vehicle at which he was, unfortunately, a master. "When I quote from the doctor's publication, he must pardon me for not giving the page, as the whole 'history' consists of only one side of a small handbill." The caustic comments grew harsher as David compared Samuel to the biblical Simon the sorcerer, called him a traitor to his earlier beliefs, and suggested that if a rift in the Association developed, then "Dr. Samuel Jones and his friends should be excluded, for we have not departed from the faith. . . ."

The use of scriptural references, quoting of historical writers, and his use of the Greek enhanced his arguments greatly, but his harsh language and ridicule of an esteemed minister was not well received by many readers. Instead of helping to heal the dispute, the controversy was widened. However, with the completion of the book and the new limestone meetinghouse, David left for a six-week trip to Ohio and a visit to his son, Morgan, who was settled on the Grave Creek property. In his absence, another son, Horatio, supplied the pulpit at the new meetinghouse at Great Valley.

On his return, he found Ann in a worsened condition, and so David remained close to home and local pastoral duties. Many found him to be a righteous, straightforward minister who brooked no bad habits or immorality. Yet others with weaknesses discovered a forgiving pastor. James Abrahams, for example, was censured by the church for hauling hay on Sunday and for excessive drinking. Witnesses were present at the church business meeting to testify against Abrahams, but Pastor Jones asked for more time to counsel with the offender before the church withdrew communion, their usual disciplinary action. When Abrahams was reported drunk again, David secretly brought him to his own house, out of reach of censorious deacons and members. As the man gradually defeated his drinking problem, his family was more than a little grateful to their long-suffering pastor. David explained that he had seen soldiers do strange things under the influence of alcohol, and he didn't want his parishioners to be expelled without every opportunity to repent.

Sickness continued to plague the Jones home. Young David was growing weak, with a deep respiratory ailment to compound his near-total blindness. He passed all his medical exams with brilliant marks, but obviously he could never practice his profession. Ann was bed-ridden, incapable of caring for herself. As young David's and Ann's conditions worsened, David remained by their sides. One day in the early spring of 1809, Ann asked David to shut her door. He sat down by her side on the bed as she took both of his hands in hers.

"David, there is something I want to say," she began.

"Don't try to speak; you're tired, Annie."

"No, I have something to say." She tried to sit up as David pushed an extra pillow behind her back.

"I want to tell you something that is obvious; you know it, but I have to say it for my own peace of mind." She looked deeply into his eyes so that he could not escape the meaning and intensity of what was to come. Her upper lip began quivering. David hurt for her struggling emotions.

"I want you to know that I love you, David Jones." She broke into tears.

"No, Annie, don't please. . . ."

"No, David. Let me speak. I want you to know that I'm sorry for all my pouting and feeling sorry for myself when you've been gone. I made things difficult for you."

"Annie . . ."

"No, I am going to speak. But this one time, David, I want to look into your eyes and tell you this—I know you've been high-strung; I know you've always been nervous to go somewhere; I know you've been blunt; and some say you're crude and outspoken. But, David Jones, you're a good man, a talented man, and I think you're the most wonderful husband a woman could ever have. I love you more than I can say, but I do love you with all my heart."

Tears streamed down David's cheeks as he wanted to protest; he wanted to repent of the loneliness he had caused her, to apologize, but he couldn't speak. He took her in his arms with a tenderness and meaning unknown to young lovers. In less than a week, he stood by her graveside, only a few feet from the Great Valley Church. His thoughts were of a laughing girl in red ribbons, of a young mother holding his child, of a woman saying "welcome home," of an older, sick wife saying, "You're the best husband . . . I love you more than I can say. . . ." "Thank you, God," David muttered aloud as his children and grandchildren pressed close to his side.

The old man rested for a few weeks before resuming his pastoral duties. His black hair showed more gray now, and his high cheekbones seemed even more prominent as his thin body grew thinner. He kept up his duties, however, and when he was asked to preach at St. David's Church on July 4, 1809, for the reinterment of his old commander, Anthony Wayne, he accepted eagerly. Hundreds crowded the church as the burial was combined with the nation's birthday celebration in Chester County. The newspapers called him "the old man eloquent" the next day and reported that many had to climb into trees to get a glimpse of the old soldier wearing a queue, cockade hat, and black trousers with silver knee and shoe buckles.

Young David died in 1811, even as his father gained physical and emotional strength. The British renewed their impressment of American seamen as well as their encouragement of western Indians against American pioneers. David wrote a series of articles about his wide knowledge of past Indian affairs in the *Philadelphia Aurora*. In a frenetic pace, he wrote two books excoriating those who advocated infant baptism. The old sarcasm burst forth in more violent expressions, and he heaped scorn on those who dared to disagree with him. He exchanged letters with President Madison following a brief visit to the White House with his former Revolutionary friend. He advocated war with the British to all who would listen. Feeling more active as international tensions increased, he took a last trip to Ohio in the summer of 1811, preaching at every opportunity. At seventy-five years of age, thin, but with sparkling eye and clear voice, he thought he was forty years old again. When war was declared with Great Britain on June 18, 1812, David rode his horse to Washington, D.C., the new capital, and, in a conversation with President Madison and Secretary of War General John Armstrong, volunteered as an army chaplain. Incredibly, they accepted his offer.

David's old verve returned to full flower as he prepared to embark on yet another military campaign. Rheumatism and stomach disorders could not depress the excitement he felt at doing his part in engaging the hated British once more. His affairs were put in order by the spring of 1813 when his youngest child came to visit him. Horatio was the pastor of the Baptist church in Roxbury, twelve miles from the farm. Since the time of his mother's death, Horatio was faithful to visit his father regularly.

"Do you eat cold leftovers like this all the time, Father?"

"Not too often. The neighbors bring me a hot dish once in a while, George's wife isn't a bad cook, and every Sunday I get invited to somebody's home. Besides, these old bones don't require much food."

"How's your rheumatism?"

"Getting better, Son. Better every day."

"You don't move around like you're better." His voice was not particularly pleasant. David turned to look at him.

"Do you have something in mind to say, Horatio?"

"Yes, I do. I dislike disagreeing with you, Father. Mainly because I always lose, just like everyone else." A trace of a smile creased his face as he paused.

"Well, out with it now, as if I didn't know."

"I don't want you to go off to the army. Now listen to me before you take off on your reasons. Pa, you're seventy-six years old, and you aren't well. Everybody else can see that except you. Every Baptist in these parts wants you to relax more and enjoy old friends and the meetings here. Your health just isn't going to let you live through another campaign."

"You know, Son, my mother expected me to die of asthma when I was five years old. The Ohio Indians thought for sure I was dead in '72. I've been shot at, starved, frozen, wheezed through so many asthma attacks I can't count them all, but I'm still here. I've outlived four of my own children, and I'll declare right now that I'm healthier than most of the rest of you. I just might outlive you yet."

Horatio shook his head slowly. He had heard all this many times before, and he could see he wasn't accomplishing his goal.

"But, Pa, please listen to me. Those reasons you gave are the very ones that ought to convince you that you shouldn't go off again. A human body can only take so much and yours has had more than its share. It's precisely because of what you've endured that you shouldn't go."

There was a pause. David spoke slowly and deliberately: "I know I can't keep up with the army like I used to. I know I'll have to ride in wagons instead of on horseback. My voice isn't as strong as it used to be. In fact, I don't have much to commend me to the army except one thing. That is, I'm a symbol of a long, bitter struggle against those British. I've fought those rascals for thirty-eight years. So some of those young Americans up in Canada might hear me stammer through a mediocre sermon, and maybe I'll collapse right in front of them. Yet they'll have to say to themselves that if that old chaplain can give his all against the English, then they can, too. Now that's why I'm going, Horatio."

"No, Pa. You're going because you've got the itch and the smell of a fight again."

"Well, I'm going, and if you're so concerned about me, just remember you children promised to ship my body back here if I do get killed or die. You can say, 'See, I told you so' over at the cemetery, for all I care."

Horatio bit his lips as he fought for control of his emotions.

"Pa, I've corresponded with Eleanor and Morgan and talked with Mary. We're not going to bring your body back."

A boltlike thrust shot through David's stomach as he wheeled toward his son.

"You promised! You all promised!" he shouted.

"We're breaking our promise now. We don't think you should go. We are all in agreement." He lowered his head.

The old man felt he was going to be sick. He leaned on the vegetable counter for support as he looked out the window away from his son. He saw orchards he and Ann had planted together. He saw the south field ploughed and planted. Ann's smokehouse was off to the left. Every tree, every arbor, every bush reminded him of the one who lay in the Great Valley cemetery, just four miles away. His voice was positive, though shaky, as he spoke softly.

"I'd always imagined lying beside your mother one day. I thought we'd be resurrected together in that place special to us. It's beautiful there in the valley." He paused as Horatio closed his eyes. "But I can't bring my own body back. I never thought I'd die in Canada, but so be it. Let them bury me where I fall because I *AM* going. I think Annie would understand, even if my children don't."

He turned to face Horatio, having regained his composure. Horatio recognized the set jaw he had seen so often before.

"You're really going on, even if we won't bring your body back?"

"You heard me, and you know I mean it. You tell your brothers and sisters that, too."

Horatio's face slowly contorted in anguish. He wept unashamedly as David stood watching him. He spoke in halting words between sobs: "Oh, Pa . . . Oh, dear Pa . . . do you really . . . do you really think we wouldn't bury you with Ma? Oh, Pa . . . of course we'll bring you back. We were only . . . we were only trying to convince . . . you not to go. We were only trying to get you to . . . we wanted you here . . . but if you were absolutely determined . . . if you went on anyhow . . . yes, Pa, I was only trying to get you to stay. . . . We love you, Pa. . . . We'll bury you with Ma. . . . We were only trying to trick you into staying. . . ."

David patted Horatio's shoulder for several minutes. "Thank you, Son. Now, you tell your brothers and sisters I'm going."

William Walley drove David to Philadelphia where the old soldier rode in a stagecoach to New Brunswick over the "worst road in the world." He sat with two men and facing three others as they bounced over the rough New Jersey countryside. David steadied himself by holding onto a cane wedged hard to the floor in front of him. After introductions, a lively political discussion ensued as to the propriety of war with England. Four of the men angrily criticized Madison's administration for causing the conflict. Another man felt that Great Britain should be defeated once and for all. David remained sullenly silent. The discussion waxed on and on, and as it did, one young lawyer increased his scathing remarks toward President Madison and all Jeffersonians. He would have done well to drop the discussion and leave David out of the fast-flowing opinions.

"A weak administration, a miserably weak administration. Jefferson and his French sympathizers were bad enough, but now this. But for this poor administration, we could be at peace with our sister country. Well, Reverend, you haven't said much. Don't you agree with me?" the lawyer queried.

"Yes, sir, I do," said David, nodding his head vigorously. "This is a weak administration, a miserably weak administration. If President Madison were half the man he ought to be," he looked straight into the eyes of the young attorney, "he would long ago have hung scores of confounded Tories such as you."

The other men in the coach stared at David incredulously, scarcely believing their ears. The discussion was over political disagreements, not threats of death. Surely, they thought, he would soften his accusations. They didn't know David.

"That's right, the name 'Tory' in time of war is traitor, and I've helped dispatch quite a few of that kind of traitor," David said.

"Who are you?" demanded the lawyer.

"I'm an old soldier who has fought the British twice before you were born, and I'm on my way north to fight the murderous barbarians again."

"Sir, if you weren't an old man, you wouldn't have the courage to speak to me like this."

"Oh, is that right? Well, let me tell you, young Tory, if I were not an old man, your traitorous body would be lying ten miles back down the road."

"If you persist in talking to me like this, I might decide you're not too old to slap, Reverend."

David's face flushed as he grabbed his cane at the end and swung at the lawyer. The other men blocked the cane as the Tory drew back with eyes and mouth wide open. When peace was restored, David, as usual, had the last word: "Any time you want to slap this old man, he won't be far away, and you just might pull back a broken arm." The remainder of the trip was passed in stony silence.

As usual, David looked up Baptists in each town and village where he spent a night. A sufficient congregation assembled after dinner in Utica to have an enjoyable worship service. David arrived at Buffalo on June 9, immediately crossing the Niagara River as he sought to join the invading American army engaged in hot pursuit of a British unit west of Toronto. When he did meet with General Dearborn's troops, the fight was over, and he preached to two thousand troops with considerable hoarseness on Sunday, June 13. At the conclusion of his prayer following the sermon, the men gave David three spontaneous cheers "for the great old chaplain." His renown as a dedicated chaplain preceded him, a fact that greatly pleased him. Whether it was due to his difficulty at having his aging voice heard, or for some other reason, David developed a method of having drummers stand in front of him as he preached to troops during the War of 1812. Drumming rolls to summon the troops, the drummers also beat quick beats on their instruments whenever David felt the men might be lapsing into sleep or disinterestedness. His presentation was not routine, to be sure.

Naval battles for control of Lake Ontario caused David's unit to be transferred to Sackets Harbor on the east shore of the lake. On the sultry shores of Lake Ontario, David developed a deep chest cough and diarrhea. He preached with great difficulty to a small congregation at the courthouse in mid-July, but he was not well. He traveled inland to Watertown to recuperate and recovered sufficient strength to have a public debate with a Unitarian a week later. He was summoned back to Sackets Harbor in August to perform that most odious of duties, ministering to a condemned man at an execution.

George Irvine was sentenced to be hanged for desertion, and though he had been a good soldier, David recorded his personality as "rash and inconsiderate." The commander, Brigadier General Lewis, would not commute the sentence, and so David preached a short message at the gallows, prayed, and then walked down the stairs, standing close by as the hood was drawn over Irvine's head. In a repetition of the pardon by General Wayne of the two condemned men in 1795, Major General James Wilkinson ordered a reduced sentence read just before the trapdoor was released.

This time, however, there was no rejoicing, since Irvine apparently lost his senses. Losing complete control of the situation, he tried to run in panic. The slack in the rope around his neck allowed him only two steps, and then he came tumbling off the side of the platform with rope, tied hands, and hood directly on top of David. His head jerked grotesquely to one side as David was sent sprawling. Quickly jumping to his feet, David grabbed Irvine's legs at the knees and pushed upward with all his might. When help arrived, David fell to the ground exhausted. Irvine lived, though, thanks to the quick-thinking old chaplain.

Admiral Perry's great victory over the British on Lake Erie was announced at Sackets Harbor on September 23, and David asked for, and received, a leave of absence to return home for the winter. His battle with diarrhea was fought with medicines, rest, and bathing in the waters of Saratoga Springs, but to little avail. He slowly became aware of the fact that he had only a limited time for further activity as a chaplain. His children and friends greeted him at home in October, careful to avoid any discussion of his possible return to the war. It was well they did not, for after a quiet winter, David left again for the northern fighting front in early May.

An important event delayed his return briefly, however. The Eleventh Continental Battalion of the Revolutionary War celebrated its thirty-sixth anniversary of the Battle of Monmouth Court House on June 8, 1814, choosing for their speaker one of the few Revolutionary War veterans still active, Chaplain David Jones. David's addresses to secular groups, as well as to religious gatherings, had a great appeal to a wide variety of listeners as he mixed large doses of patriotism with remembrances of spectacular events and associations with great people. Through the message at Monmouth Court House, he also pronounced jeremiads and prophecies of doom on their persistent enemy, Great Britain. A long standing ovation greeted his concluding remarks, and many of the old veterans had tear-stained eyes as their old comrade climbed into a carriage and rode off to yet another campaign.

Sporadic fighting was flaring around Fort George and Lewistown on the Canadian side of the Niagara River as David neared Buffalo.

He hurried to the ferry and joined other soldiers nervously navigating dangerous whirlpools as they pushed on to join the fighting. A hard rain beat down on the group while they were forced to march hard to join the fight. The seventy-seven-year-old chaplain expended almost all his physical resources as he walked with the younger men. They joined the rear guard and laid their packs and extra equipment down, continuing on into the battle which raged only a mile away. David's muscles were twitching with exhaustion; he felt faint. Through blurred vision he watched the men march toward the smoke, dust, booming cannon, and cracking rifles. He desperately wanted to go with them, but he sagged slowly to the ground, instead, on a pile of packs nearby. He had come as close as he ever would to his last military battle.

A Colonel Wilcox found him lying there several hours later, his clothes and boots soaking wet, and the old man too ill to move. Calling a surgeon, Colonel Wilcox gathered blankets for him and ordered a private to find a horse and take him to the field hospital near Lewistown. After two days of rest with the wounded and sick, David became restless to move somewhere. When permission to leave was not granted by the surgeon, David packed his saddlebags and left while the doctors were busy with their other patients. It was twenty miles to Buffalo, and with the saddlebags slung over his shoulder, he determined he could make the trip in two or three days. Fortunately, a wagon overtook him toward sundown of the first day, just before he collapsed of exhaustion.

It was clear now, even to David, that his usefulness as a chaplain was at an end. He had contracted a deep chest cold, and his diarrhea continued to plague and weaken him. He headed away from the battle area, at last, to Saratoga Springs near Albany. There, after recuperating for a few days, he wrote a series of four lengthy letters to the president, reporting on the war, suggesting strategy, and appraising the generals he had met. If he couldn't fight, he would write, he told himself. He was not completely senile, however, as he noted in his diary that perhaps his frequent letters to Madison, Monroe, Armstrong, and Wilkinson were "a few more than acceptable."

He then began his final trip home. As he worked his way south toward Pennsylvania, he found opportunity and energy to dispute with "infant baptizers" and to preach when he was able. The speaking and disputing became less frequent, however, as he left New York

City for the final leg of his journey across New Jersey. He arrived at Horatio's house on Saturday night, and though his son pleaded with him to remain there for several days, David was most anxious to get to his own home and bed. He rode twelve miles through a pouring rain while Horatio and his family were at church the next day. His family were beside themselves with worry when they returned home and found him gone. But by then, David was easing himself off Horatio's horse in his own barn.

As the days and weeks passed, David's mind told him that he was feeling better, but his body became increasingly less mobile. The venerable chaplain sat in the parlor during the days, reading his Bible and entertaining guests who came to call on him. Against the advice of his family, he roused himself for one last public appearance on September 20, 1817, the fortieth anniversary of the Paoli "massacre." A ten-foot-high monument was to be dedicated on that day in commemoration of the Americans who had fallen on that spot long ago. A white stone wall capped with a painted maple rail surrounded the monument and the graves of forty victims of the night attack. Two large cannons were placed in front of the monument, and a large reviewing stand was built a few feet north of the seats set up for the crowd.

The West Chester Federalist and the *Philadelphia Aurora* reported that a huge throng attended the event to catch a glimpse of the eloquent old chaplain. He was described as a "tall, erect, soldierly looking figure who, two years more than fourscore years have shed their snows on his venerable head." He was assisted to the podium by a Major John Barnard and J. Pearce, Esquire, where he gave a detailed account of the attack and closed his brief address by exhorting the crowd to faithful patriotism, and, of course, a warning against the "machinations of the British."

There was no specific cause for David's increased feebleness, only the accumulation of the many years of active life. His second daughter, Mary, moved into the Easttown farmhouse to care for her father, while her husband, Archibald McLean, worked the farm. Eleanor, with an astute sense of business, took over the family finances after her husband died, and in the summer of 1819 assisted her father in making his will. He listed his four pieces of property, clothing, furniture, and personal items, giving them to children, grandchildren, and friends.

Horatio visited his father each week during memorable days for

David. Sitting together with Horatio, Eleanor, Mary, and their mates, and surrounded by several grandchildren, they talked by the big fireplace in the parlor far into the nights, recounting their favorite stories. He never regretted his beliefs or his actions, and so he lived his last days free of doubts, as completely happy and content as a human can be. No one suggested the sessions end until David's head gradually rested in sleep against the big pillow of his rocker. In the autumn of 1819, the gatherings moved out into the sunshine as David smiled happily at his grandchildren's games and at the loving care of his children. He became too ill to join in family dinners during the winter, and as the new year arrived, he lapsed into long, unnatural periods of sleep. In the late afternoon of February 5, he asked to be helped to his chair by the fireplace where he slipped out of this life without his children noting any pain or discomfort whatever. He simply went to sleep and never awakened.

He was buried on February 7 in the cemetery at the Baptist Church in the Great Valley beside his wife. A large flat gravestone reads:

This tablet records a brief memorial of the Rev. Dr. David Jones, many years pastor of the Baptist Church in the Great Valley. He departed this life February 5, 1820, aged 83 years, 8 months, and 13 days, possessing a strong mind and a complete education. He was

*David Jones' grave at the
Baptist Church in the Great Valley*

distinguished in the various spheres he filled. Glowing with an ardent love for his country, he served her in the Revolutionary contest as Chaplain, which station he also filled in the contest with the savages and in the War of 1812. His love to the Republic remained undiminished while life continued. As a divine with undeviating devotion, he advocated the doctrines of Christianity published by Jesus Christ and his Apostles and embraced by venerable reformers. As a Christian for sixty years, his motto was "by their fruits ye shall know them," an adherence to which was exemplified in his protracted and Religious course. In his death Christianity has lost an able advocate, society a useful member and the Commonwealth one of its founders. Here moulders his body, his soul has winged its way to God and heard the glorious welcome, "Well done, good and faithful servant, enter thou into the joy of your Lord."

Bibliographical Note

Many people and institutions were helpful in providing the sources of existing manuscripts of and about David Jones. Without their aid, thorough research would have been impossible.

Rev. Edward C. Starr, Curator of the American Baptist Historical Society in Rochester, New York, made two diaries, a memoir, twenty-six manuscript letters, and several secondary sources available to me from his organization.

Mr. Gary Christopher, of the Historical Society of Pennsylvania in Philadelphia, was helpful in directing me to a diary, several letters, and other miscellaneous papers of Jones'.

A full and descriptive genealogy of the Jones-Morgan-Griffith family, together with the early church records of the Welsh Tract Baptist Church were read at the Historical Society of Delaware at Wilmington.

The Library of Congress and National Archives in Washington, D.C., contain numerous sources for a study of Chaplain Jones, particularly the James Madison correspondence.

Each church where Jones was a member has extant records of church business and history during his lifetime. In addition to the Welsh Tract records, the Hopewell Baptist Church and Hopewell Museum in New Jersey provided interesting material about the Hopewell Baptist Academy. The First Baptist Church of Middletown, New Jersey, Rev. Herbert H. Mardis, pastor, allowed me the use of their library and records. Crosswicks Baptist Church (now First Baptist Church of Imlaystown, New Jersey) has the original records of the church. Pastor Allen Garvie and Mr. and Mrs. Frank Polhenus were most kind to allow me a visit to the Old Yellow Meeting House at Crosswicks and to provide me with the records. The Southampton Baptist Church records were read after much effort and the help of Dr. Ruth Ross and Mr. Horace Lefferts. Rev.

Chester Winters, pastor of The Baptist Church in the Great Valley and local historian, was extremely helpful with my research in and around Devon, Pennsylvania.

Mr. and Mrs. David Cornog, of Wayne, Pennsylvania, own a portrait and several items of memorabilia of Mr. Cornog's ancestor, David Jones. Their friendship and aid was most appreciated.

This research was used in another, more scholarly, writing—a dissertation for the Doctor of Philosophy degree at the University of Colorado.

A special word of gratitude is due Dr. Norman Maring of Eastern Baptist Theological Seminary for his encouragement and direction and Dr. George Pilcher, my advisor at Colorado, who originally encouraged me to delve further into the study of "my friend David."